QUAE NOVA; NEW WORLDS OF ENGLISH LITERATURE

DR. SARAN S.

Contents

Contents

Foreword

Dr. Jinu George
Member, PG Board of Studies & Research Guide
(MG University, Kottayam)
Associate Professor, Dept. English
St. Peter's College, Kolenchery

Owing to the preponderance of the variety of pedagogical topics on research theories dealt with this catalytic volume titled 'Quae Nova; New Worlds of English Literature' will ultimately be relished by every genre of Linguistic and literary scholastic community. The multi-faceted analytical framework of the book makes it an immensely readable volume that elaborates on various processes of assimilation. In theme and treatment, every chapter carries an esoteric reflection holding a mirror up to the sparsely delineated issues such as Identity, Geospatial and Digital Humanities, Media and connoisseur ethics, development-oriented planes of communication, Ideological roaming over eco- cultural studies as well as eco-critical investigations, value centred mediations on post-modern narratives fantasy - fiction etc...

Apart from introducing prominent pedagogic linkages that corroborate diverse perspectives such as that of language, writing, and evaluation - a compact study on the data analysis framework also has been meticulously endeavoured in the volume wholesomely. The author outlines explore, defines draws us into the essence of linguistic struggles with issues regarding environment, ethos, habitats and historicity.

The volume throws (casts) an ambient aura on rarely attempted linguistic and pedagogic realms such as the stereotypical faiths and ideologies embedded in the postmodern vis-à-vis postcolonial fiction writing. In a syllogistic survey on morality, culture and gender roles that are resplendent in 21st century Neo- Feminism, New-wave cellulosic parameters has been earnestly decoded and deciphered in the pattern of set evaluation, rendering a brilliant exposition.

Moreover, this journal provides pathfinding reasons for avid minds that aspire to sharpen their skills in the arena of audio-visual media. A punctilious reference has been rendered on eco-critical studies which is the amalgam of literature and environment from the multidisciplinary as well as interdisciplinary point of view where all sciences appear 'randomized' to seek out solutions for global issues that threaten sustenance of life and longevity of habitats.

The book could surely be estimated as a beacon light of scholastic reason and pedagogical catechism which could in no way be considered as a cavalcade for cursory perusal. Dabbling into the profound ocean of innovated and updated ideologies, any ambitious diver could emerge from the depths with pearls and emeralds if attempted in a quintessential and dedicated reading mode as Leopold Bloom had suggested.

Since the topics are having interred continual relevance, the book in every sense stands head and shoulders above its peers regarding a theme, treatment and above all, the sterling information it offers. Ardently scanning the book, an ambitious scholar will undoubtedly have the ecstasy of capturing the iridescence of novel ideas regarding creative notions about the methodology and application of linguistic patterns in Post-modern narrative as well as the Post-Covid Digital era narrative where the cornucopia of Media literacy has opened vast portals for flamboyant writing mandates.

The diligent yeomen efforts were undertaken by the editor in this daring venture of rejuvenating diverse psycholinguistics and pedagogic perspectives aptly deserve laudatory claps and praises since he had sincerely endeavoured to enliven the rarely frequented scholastic realms, which would otherwise have faded into oblivion. My whole-hearted cheers for his innovative assay trying to maintain a galaxy of creative and motivational principles radiant on the horizon of pedagogy, by pushing away the clouds of darkness.

I wish a host of English language aspirants might take their ambitions undertaking a reliable pathfinder.

The book could surely be estimated as a beacon light of scholastic reason and pedagogical catechism which could in no way be considered as a cavalcade for cursory perusal. Dabbling into the profound ocean of innovated and updated ideologies, any ambitious diver could emerge from the depths with pearls and emeralds if attempted in a quintessential and dedicated reading mode as Leopold Bloom had suggested.

Since the topics are having inferred continual relevancy, the book in every sense stands head and shoulders above its peers regarding a theme, treatment and [illegible] startling information it offers. Ardently scanning the book, an industrious scholar will undoubtedly [illegible] the ecstasy of [illegible] the endless sea of novel ideas regarding creative notions about the methodology and application of linguistic patterns in Post-modern narrative as well as the Post-Covid Digital era narrative where the [illegible] Media have [illegible] vast portals for [illegible] writing mandate.

[illegible] treatment [illegible] undertaken by the [illegible] [illegible] diverse [illegible] and [illegible] perspectives aptly deserve [illegible] sincerely [illegible] scholastic [illegible], which would otherwise have faded into oblivion. [illegible] for his innovative essay trying to [illegible] principles [illegible] in the horizon of pedagogy by pushing away the clouds of darkness.

I wish a host of English language aspirants might take their ambitions undertaking a reliable pathfinder.

Editor

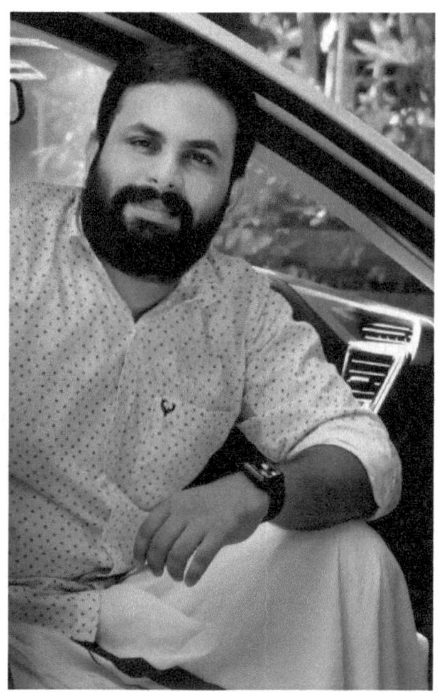

Dr. Saran S.
Assistant Professor & Head
Department of English
University Institute of Technology
Pathiyoor Regional Centre
University of Kerala, Thiruvananthapuram

Dr. Saran S., is a writer, Poet, Nature Activist, Teacher, and Research Scholar. He completed his Doctoral Research at the Department of English, M. S. University in 2020. Currently, he is working as an Assistant Professor and Head in the Department of English, University Institute of Technology Pathiyoor, University of Kerala. His areas are Comparative Literature, Cultural Studies, Film Studies, Psychoanalytical Studies and Eco Studies. He is the author of several articles published in various national and international journals as well as six academic books on topics of current interest like English Language, Film Studies, Partition Studies and Cultural Studies. He also authored a collection of poems and short stories. He also edited twenty-three international books. He is the chief editor of Edit Academic, an advisory board member and Associate Editor in *The Creative Launcher*, international, open access, peer-reviewed refereed, e-journal in English and also an Editorial Board Member in *Shodhkosh: Journal of Visual and Performing Arts* (UGC-Care Listed Journal).

Contributors

1. "Narrating Female Bildung" - *__Dr. Lalitha Sarma R.__, Assistant Professor in English, Department of Humanities and Social Sciences, C. V. Raman Global University, Bhubaneswar.

2. "English Language Teaching" - *__Dr. Maheshkumar Shankar Kedar__, Assistant Professor at Sinhgad College of Science, Ambegaon(Bk), Pune.

3. "Fantasies of A Make Belief World: An Analysis on the Influence of Cartoons, a Visual Medium on Children" - *__Joshna Francis__, Assistant Professor, Department of English, Bhavan's College of Arts & Commerce, Kakkanad.

4. "The Feminist Relooking of Kavitha Kane in Fictionalising *Ramayana* and *Mahabharata*" - *__Meera K. S.__, Assistant Professor, Department of English, Sree Mahadeva College, Vaikom, Kottayam.

5. "Adjunction of Actor-Network Theory and Science Fiction in Posthumanism" - *__Sali S.__, Assistant Professor, Post-Graduate Department of English, Don Bosco Colleg, Kottiyam, Kerala.

6. "Representation of Gender in Women Magazines Covers; a Study Based on Vanitha Magazine" - *__Jishnu D.__, Research Scholar, Department of Media and Communication, Central University of Tamil Nadu, Thiruvarur. ** __Jishnu Nampoothiri P. J.__, Assistant Professor (on contract) Sree Ayyappa College, Eramllikkara, Chengannur. ***__Shamala R.__, Assistant Professor, Department of Media and Communication, Central University of Tamil Nadu, Thiruvarur.

7. "Bapsi Sidhwa's *The Pakistani Bride*: A Feminist Study" - *__Devika Singh__., Ph. D. Research Scholar, Central

University of Haryana.

8. "The Other Side of Multiculturalism: Violence in Gloria Naylor's *The Women of Brewster Place*" - ***Ms. Aashlesha. V. Lele**

9. "A Study on Myth and Narration in *Naga-Mandala*" - ***Ann Hermina Christy, **Suryanarayana Menon** & *****Sachin S.**, University Institute of Technology, Pathiyoor Regional Centre, Department of English, University of Kerala.

10. "Trauma and its Manifestations in *The Kite Runner*" - ***Asha Krishnan, **Siyana Sulaiman, ***Ashid,** & ******Anshad**, University Institute of Technology, Pathiyoor Regional Centre, Department of English, University of Kerala.

11. "Digital Learning and Pedagogical Implication in Covid-19 Pandemic Times" - ***Nandini Jyothira**,Teacher Educant, Mahatma Gandhi University, Alappuzha, Kerala.

Introduction

Numerous nations, including the United Kingdom and its royal dependencies, the Republic of Ireland, the United States, and the former British Empire nations, are represented in English-language literature. More than 1,400 years have passed since the beginning of the English language. Old English refers to the earliest varieties of English, a collection of Anglo-Fresian dialects that were introduced to Great Britain by Anglo-Saxon conquerors in the fifth century. Despite being set in Scandinavia, Beowulf is the most well-known book in Old English and has attained national epic status in England. The written form of the Anglo-Saxon language, however, declined in use after the Norman conquest of England in 1066.

French replaced English as the primary language of courts, parliament, and polite society as a result of the influence of the emerging nobility. Middle English refers to the English that was used after the Norman invasion. This kind of English persisted until the 1470s when the London-based Chancery Standard (late Middle English) took over. The Canterbury Tales author Geoffrey Chaucer (1343–1400) played a pivotal role in the acceptance of Middle English as a legitimate literary language at a time when French and Latin were still the two most common literary languages in England. The King James Bible (1611), the Great Vowel Shift, and Johannes Gutenberg's creation of the printing press in 1439 all contributed to the linguistic standardisation of the language.

Introduction

Numerous nations, including the United Kingdom and its royal dependencies, the Republic of Ireland, the United States, and the former British Empire nations, are represented in English-language literature. More than 1,400 years have passed since the beginning of the English language. Old English refers to the earliest varieties of English, a collection of Anglo-Frisian dialects that were introduced to Great Britain by Anglo-Saxon conquerors in the 5th century. Despite being [illegible] in Scandinavia, Beowulf [illegible] the most well-known book in Old English and has attained national epic status in England. The written form of the Anglo-Saxon language, however, declined in use after the Norman conquest of England in 1066.

French replaced English as the primary language of [illegible] as a result of the [illegible] the [illegible] Middle English refers to [illegible] Norman conquest [illegible] when [illegible] London [illegible] (Middle English) took over [illegible] French [illegible] the emergence of Modern English [illegible] literary language at a time [illegible] still the two most common [illegible] the King James Bible (1611), the Great Vowel Shift, and Johannes Gutenberg's creation of the printing press in 1450 all contributed to the linguistic standardization of the language.

CHAPTER I

NARRATING FEMALE BILDUNG

Dr. Lalitha Sarma R.
Assistant Professor in English
Department of Humanities and Social Sciences
C. V. Raman Global University, Bhubaneswar

INTRODUCTION

All issues that fall within the portfolio of Gender Studies are reducible to the problem of *difference. The difference* appears as hierarchical binary opposition in dominant order and is structured in pairs of fundamental dualities such as mind and body, culture and nature, reason and imagination, and man and woman. In the existing patriarchal system, structured on this binary thinking, the masculine constitutes the norm, the positive, whereas the woman is an aberration, the negative. She is defined in relation to what man is not, as "lack," of not being a man. Having no identity of her own, she often serves as an empty space, upon which he may project his desires within the stipulations of the existing and permitted system. In her oft-quoted words, Simone de Beauvoir pointed out the issue of how men see women as "the Other:" She is 'incidental, the inessential as opposed to the essential. He is the subject, he is the Absolute — she is the other' (Rajni Walia, 3).

Narrating Female Bildung

The question of *difference* is not merely one of having a man as the referent or exploring how a woman is different from a man. It is also about seeing women as 'flat embodiments of a particular force or theme,' and 'mythically, allegorically, symbolically, but never realistically as fully rounded complex human beings,' (Rajni Walia, 3) i.e., the *difference* is also about how different women are from what men think they are. As Gayle Greene and Coppélia Kahn remark, in their essay "Feminist Scholarship and the Social Construction of Woman," more is involved than the bifurcated comprehension of experience: the dichotomization of masculine and feminine in terms of such polarities as 'culture and nature, 'truth and duplicity', 'reason and passion', 'day and night' – the terms associated with the female always requiring control by the superior male. Thus the meaning of gender in patriarchal ideology is '*not* simply "difference", but...division, oppression, inequality, interiorized inferiority for women' (Barret 1980, pp 112-13) (Green and Kahn, 3-4).

Feminist studies aim at remodelling the desiderata of society. They focus on the inscription of the female subject in culture and expose the ways in which the 'universal,' 'humanistic' principle is almost always contradicted both in terms of textual violation and sexual violence. In its strategy of deconstructing the mechanisms of patriarchy in creating a cultural mindset, feminist literary studies set out on a two-pronged attack on the existing system that involved exposing the male versions of the world, and exploring the nature of the female outlook, as well as reconstructing the lost and suppressed records of feminine experience. The endeavour is to liberate women from those established structures and cultural constructs that persistently marginalise and inform the 'feminine.' The discovery, reconstruction and reconstitution of the idea of the female subject can be done only through a study of the deep-rooted leitmotifs and themes that manifest in literary works as a narrative strategy, various temporal and spatial metaphors, linguistic patterns and, most importantly, thematic design.

'Women Narratives of Self Empowerment is crucial because they depict the feminine *bildung* or 'the internal life of female characters in the process of self-discovery' (Greene and Kahn, 48). Collating such sagas of feminine self-search would help us ascertain if there indeed is a recurrent pattern or universality in woman's experience, an interface sans cultural context, sans linguistic or regional divide or sans all "shadow lines."

Psychoanalysis is a useful tool for feminists because of its psychological definition of gender. It makes diverse inroads in the efforts of feminist scholarship to challenge and change the tradition that has long silenced and marginalised women. It does so by deconstructing predominantly male paradigms and reconstructing a female perspective and experience. In feminist literary studies, psychoanalysis provides assistance by studying the psychodynamics of female characters and their authors, deriving the psychoanalytic patterns of textual metaphor, and eliciting patterns from the psychodynamics of gendered readings. It investigates the interaction of conscious and unconscious elements in the collective mind and gleans out the specific features of difference such as gender perspective and point of view, gender subjectivity in representations of displacement, and gender 'absence,' involving reading against the grain of the text.

Feminist psychoanalytic criticism aims at discovering the processes of gender difference. Critics have also observed that consciousness-raising in feminist groups is akin to the bringing up of the repressed into consciousness in therapy or the hoisting of the sub-text in literary criticism: all these are ways of learning about the previously unexpressed effects of patriarchy. In its functions as a political movement and as literary practice, feminism is analogous to psychoanalysis in the use of the model of repression. Woman's experience is often held as repressed or as embedded in the 'unconscious.' Diane Purkiss, in "Women's Rewriting of Myth," remarks:

> Since Freud and Jung alike represented myths as part of the masculine cultural unconscious, femininity was constructed as the unconscious of the unconscious, the dark continent of the dark continent (Irigaray, 1985; Grosz, 1990). In psychoanalysis, a crucial notion is that the return of what has been repressed or silenced has the power to undo the stable constructions of identity and culture built on its repression (see Mitchell, 1974).... The return of the feminine has the power to shake male culture by undoing its central logic. (Larrington, 448)

An understanding of the cultural inheritance and the collective unconscious that operates in people's minds comprises 'myth.' 'Myth' is etymologically derived from the Greek word '*mythos*,' meaning word, speech, story, or legend. Myths are not just stories of primordial, universal events. They are made and remade, enacted and distilled, in contemporary times, in an individual's mind. Carolyne Larrington, states in the "Introduction" to *TheFeminist Companion to Mythology*:

> Myth furnishes us with more than a repertoire of literary plots and themes, however. Mythology, the study of myth, introduces us to new ways of looking at social structures so that we can examine constants and variables in the organization of human society, in particular ... women's role across different cultures and historical periods....Within the study of mythology, female figures

have too often been reviewed reductively, purely in terms of their sexual function and thus confined in a catch-all category labelled fertility....Women need to know the myths which have determined both how we see ourselves and how society regards us. (Larrington, ix)

Thus, myth is a key term in feminist discourse. Much of mythology passes down into the oral tradition. Whatever is handed down, from one generation to another, is preserved, but it still undergoes change. We see that, across cultures, myths lay great emphasis on feminine virtue, chastity and sacrifice. A clear dichotomy may be perceived in the inscription of the female subject in culture and myth. Alongside the celebration and portrayal of woman as a deity, and 'mother', she is also viewed as 'Kaanchan Kamini,' i.e., as one who functions as a seductive figure, arousing passion. This inherent contradiction is the finest instance of the unstable signification of woman that pervades the socio-cultural, mythic-poetic strata. In Indian spiritual parlance, a woman is revered as an embodiment of 'power', as a universal mother. But, she is also equated to death and feared as the ultimate pitfall in a pilgrim's progress. Though myths project women as powerful, they are always considered secondary. Women are presented in stereotyped, restricted roles. Psychoanalytic studies of women's narratives unravel certain archetypes that recurrently appear in myths and legends. Myths embedded in feminist narratives hold a crucial role in the study of the psychic development of the feminine and the feminine development of the psyche.

Where Shall We Go This Summer? by Anita Desai is a powerful novel replete with inherent complexities and contradictions that give much scope for psychoanalytic study. The protagonist of the novel, Sita is in some sense a victim of psychological oppression. Unlike her mythical namesake, who refuses to reconcile with her husband after rejection when she is in the family way, Desai's pregnant-for-the-fifth-time Sita decides to go away from her husband Raman in order to confront herself. Whereas the Sita of Ramayana feels completely lost on her separation from her husband, but later grows into a woman character of great power when she refuses to undergo a second test to prove her chastity just to unite with her husband, Sita Desai's novel is almost a retraction of such feminist idealism. She undermines the glory associated with 'motherhood' by refusing to accept her biological role. The 'paranoiac show of rage, fear, and revolt,' (Desai, 20) 'the drama of her distress' (Desai, 23) result from the disillusionment with her faith in motherhood and nurturance. She comes to believe that 'The creative impulse had no chance, against the overpowering desire to destroy' (Desai, 30). Her horror is on account of the realisation that 'destruction came so naturally' (Desai, 30). She feels that -

By giving birth to the child now so safely contained, would she be performing an act of creation or, by releasing it in violent, pain-wracked blood-bath, would she only be destroying what was, at the moment, safely contained and perfect? More and more she lost all feminine, all maternal belief in childbirth, all faith in it, and began to fear it as yet one more act of violence and murder in a world that had more of them in it than she could take (Desai, 38).

Initially, she feels the need to move away from her husband and go to the haven of Manori. Unlike the ideal of liberated feminist heroines, Sita has no control over her reproductive abilities. Frustrated by her inability to cope with the pressures of her world, she hopes to run away from the terrifying ennui that defines her. But she realizes that she cannot keep the baby within her, but has to let it be born. The unborn baby represents the stereotype of a woman that society forces the woman to deliver when she is actually not so. She is unable to retain certain things that she does not wish to divulge. But since escapism is no truce with reality, latent must eventually surface. Under a destiny imposed upon her from outside for centuries together, women have reduced them to what they are.

A beautiful contrast to this helpless paranoid pregnant woman is Mrs. Vidya Bagchi, the protagonist of the 2012 Bollywood thriller, *Kahaani*. Subverting the protocols of male-dominated Indian filmdom, the movie is a rare original with no hero, no male lead. The protagonist is a woman in advanced stages of pregnancy in search of her missing husband who arrives at Kolkata, where she is a complete stranger. If pregnancy and womanhood were held hitherto as a symbol of creative flux and delicateness, the movie is a bombshell being a reversal of roles, subverting stereotypes and disrupting clichés. The symbolism of the movie is akin to the impact of Sylvia Plath's *Edge*. Two powerful women of the classical world are simultaneously evoked in Plath's *Edge*: the enrapturing and suicidal Cleopatra, and the murderous-mother Medea. Through her poetic gesture, Plath is asserting that femininity can be perfect or complete only in the freedom to both accept and refuse 'the organization of female sexuality under patriarchy, allowing women simultaneously to act out and refuse femininity' (Larrington, 454).

The twin aspects that the woman contains, according to critics, is 'the female internalization of violence against women, and the female agent who externalizes that violence' (Larrington, 454). In *Edge*, Plath twines the two conflicting strands of thought as she 'identifies, rather than identifying with, a set of opposing stories about women's violence in relation to their bodies and their children.' (Larrington, 454) Purkiss pertinently remarks on Plath's poem and its motif of woman:

But she makes no gesture towards recuperating these stories for a socially sanctioned femininity. Rather the poem speaks from the position(s) of femininities driven out of society to be the violent other. More importantly, it refuses to take up a single position: the woman is not unequivocally either aggressor or victim, but neither and both. Plath speaks from the extreme and opposed positions they represent, the position designated as the limit, the absolute 'Edge.' The poem itself does a kind of violence to our ideas of what is appropriate, what can be said and who can say it. (Larrington, 454)

Likewise, Mrs. Bagchi's '*kahaani*' is a woman's journey to that absolute edge and subsequent entry into the interiors of the masculine hubris of society. It's a celebration of motherhood, though of a different kind: the festive air of Vijayadashami has a shade of sorrow: it is miscarriage masquerading as pregnancy. In Vidya is embodied woman in totality: woman as the creator, protector and destroyer. Even the subtle suggestion of the tinge of romance between Satyoki "Rana" Sinha, the cop and the protagonist Vidya is an outstanding advancement of our collective perspective. Though initially, it is only a rural boy's fascination of London- returnee's computer skills, gradually this hero-worship becomes an adoration coupled with protective care. The concept of a bachelor falling in love with a pregnant woman is a very forward gesture in India, even on celluloid. In a society that shuns widows as inauspicious, Arup Basu's widow walks through the Durga Puja settings, vermillion smeared on her face, draped in a *lal paad* sari symbolising marriage and auspiciousness, having fulfilled her commitment to the deceased husband.

The symbolism of Goddess Durga in slaying the evil is central to the film's tenor. The fake pregnancy and prosthetic abdomen, the 'truth' of her widowhood, and her outstanding plot of making the IB a ploy in her act of vengeance all provide us with a novel and significant model of inverting the mythical construct of woman. The film reinstates the idea of Stri as Shakti; she is no more an abala. Self-empowerment and resilience acquire a different dimensions in this context. Empowerment becomes self-discovery. Power in women is not a 'giveable' but a discoverable.

CONCLUSION

Among feminists, there is a strong emphasis on the 'constructed-ness' of universal femininity, and the influence of images and representations of femininity promulgated by literature, media and culture. The male point of view has long been accepted as the norm. Consequently, even women have come to internalise these culturally conditioned and received images of women. In order to escape typecasting in sexual identity, such conditioning has to be resisted. Gender roles must, therefore, be malleable and compliant, not inevitable and unchangeable givens. Mrs. Vidya Bagchi in Sujoy Ghosh's *Kahaani*, thus, is a powerful feminist hero who destabilises the fixities of gender, leading to fresh cultural representations. She is neither/ both the victim and the victimiser. The film is a visual and aesthetic metaphor. It is the narrative of a feminine *bildung*, a woman's quest for meaning and fulfilment; but also it is Liebestod, a mystical moment of convergence of love and death. Just as blindness is the point of breakdown of painting as an art, the character of Mrs Vidya Bagchi deconstructs our stereotype of womanhood and motherhood.

WORKS CITED

Desai, Anita. where Shall We Go This Summer? Delhi: Vihar Publishing House Pvt. Ltd., 1975.

Kahn, Gayke Greene and Coppelia, ed. Making a Difference: Feminist Literary Criticism. London: Routledge, 1985.

Larrington, Carolyne. The Feminist Companion to Mythology. London: Pandora Press, 1992.

Walia, Rajni. "Feminine self-appraisal in contemporary in contemporary women's fiction." Women and Self: Fiction of Jean Rhys, Barbara Pym, Anita Brookner. New Delhi: Books Plus, 2001. 1-4.

CHAPTER II

ENGLISH LANGUAGE TEACHING

Dr. Maheshkumar Shankar Kedar

Assistant Professor at Sinhgad College of Science Ambegaon(Bk), Pune.

INTRODUCTION

Mankind in the early ages observed other living creatures making noises to communicate their feelings. Gradually, human beings also acquired the skill of communicating a large number of things through what we now call language. Human beings alone have the complex skill of using language through speech and writing. We use our vocal organs to make different sounds, sound clusters, words, phrases and sentences.

Language is the result of evolution and convention. No language was created in a day or by a single person. It is mutually created by a group of humans to communicate. Languages also change and die, grow and expand, unlike human institutions. Every language is a convention of a community that passes down from generation to generation.

Language plays an important role in human life. We try learning and using language as a means of communication as well as a social symbol of humanity. By using the language, one can make statements, convey facts or information, explain or report something and maintain social relations. English is considered to be an international link language. It is very popular and is widely used by most people in the world. English is available to us as a historical heritage of the British Empire in addition to our own languages. We should make the best use of English to develop ourselves culturally, scientifically, technologically and materially so that we can compete with the rest of the world.

Meaning of Language

The word ‘Language’ is derived from the Latin word ‘Lingue’ which means ‘produced with the tongue’. Hence language means a thing which is produced with the tongue. Let’s see some of the definitions by linguistic.

"Language is a purely human and non-instinctive method of communicating ideas, emotions and desires by means of a system of voluntarily produced symbols." - Edward Sapir

“Language is a set of arbitrary vocal symbols by means of which a social group communicates.” - Block and Tragers

“Language is a set of human habits, the purpose of which is to give expression to human thoughts and feelings especially to impart them to others.” - Otto Jespersen

“A language is a system of arbitrary vocal symbols by means of which a social group operates.” - Bernard Bloch & George L. Trager

If we analyze all these definitions, we get a comprehensive definition of language, that is; “Language is a set of arbitrary vocal symbols by means of which a social group operates, communicates and expresses their emotions, feelings and desires.”

Characteristics of Language:-

Language is an inseparable part of human society. Human civilization has been possible only through language. Language is basically human. It is different from animal communication. Let’s look at some of the characteristics of language;

a. Language is Learnt

Language is not a born activity such as crying and walking. It is not an automatic process. It has to be learnt. Any learner learns the language by imitation and practice.

b. Language is an acquired Behaviour

Language is acquired behaviour.If a baby or man is shifted to another community or cultural group, he will acquire the language spoken by that cultural community. For example; if an Indian family is settled in the United States, the children of the family will acquire the English language with an American accent.

c. Language is a System

Language is a system like a human body, just as the body functions through different organs such as the brain, heart, and lungs. In the same way, language functions through sounds, words and structures.

d. Language is Vocal

The language is primarily observed in speech. Speech is a fundamental thing in language learning, reading and writing are secondary. Through speech and modulation of speech, we get a clear picture of English inflexion.

e. Ever-changing

No language on earth is static. Every language is undergoing changes in its grammar, vocabulary, structure and phonology over the course of time.

f. Language is for Communication

The main purpose of language is communication. Since it is so, a person's speech must be intelligible to others. For this, he must acquire the right pronunciation and intonation.

g. Language is Arbitrary

Language is arbitrary. There is no relationship between the words of a language and their meaning. The relationship between words and meaning is arbitrary.

There is no reason why a language is called 'Language' in English or 'Bhasha' in Hindi.

h. Language is based on Cultural Experiences

Every language is the product of a particular society and culture. 'Good morning', 'Thank you, 'Sorry' and such kinds of words reveal the culture of English people. In each language, there are words that show the specific culture of that community.

i. Language is Made of Habits

A person can be said to have learnt a language when he can speak it without any conscious effort. No language can be learnt without sufficient practice. A language is learnt by use and not by rules. Learning a language is a process of habit formation.

j. Language is Unique

Each language is unique. No two languages are alike. They cannot have the same set of patterns of structures, sounds, grammatical rules or words. The sounds, structures, and vocabularies of every language have their own speciality.

Functions of Language

There are seven basic functions of language which can be summarized as follows:

a. The Instrumental Function

The word 'instrumental' means serving as an instrument or means. The instrumental function refers to the use of language as an instrument to make the recipient do something. For ex: Requesting (Please, give me a glass of water. Will you do me a favour?) Commanding (Open the door Throw away this garbage) etc. It serves the function of 'I want' the satisfaction of material needs.

b. The Regulatory Function

'To regulate' means to control or to direct by a rule, method or principle. The regulatory function of language refers to the use of language to regulate the behaviour of others.

Instruction or teaching can be regarded as a type of communicative behaviour intended to cause the addressee to do something. It also includes advising and suggesting. For ex:

1. You should take some rest. (Advising)
2. You must not take things that don't belong to you. (Control through warning)
3. If you steal again I will smack you. (Control through threat)
4. You will make Mummy very unhappy if you steal again. (Control through emotional appeal)
5. Parking is not allowed. (Control through rule)

c. The Interaction Function

'To interact' means to 'to act one upon other or to talk with each other.' The interactional function of language refers to the use of language in the interaction between 'self and others. It is a 'me and you' function. It is a contact-oriented function. It includes greetings (Good Morning, Happy Diwali, Happy Eid, Congratulation), sympathy (I share your sorrow, Keep patience, Allah will help you), gratitude (Thanks a lot, Thank you for your guidance, we are grateful for your contribution), compliments (Your dress is very good. How beautiful she is!), hostility (Go to hell, Get out of here), etc.

d. The Personal Function

The word 'personal' means private or of a particular person. The personal function of language refers to the use of language to express personal feelings and meanings. It aims at a direct expression of the speaker's attitude towards what he is speaking about. For ex: A poem, a speech, an expression of love and sorrow, etc. Thus this function refers to the use of language either to express the speaker's feelings or to evoke feelings on the part of the auditor.

e. The Heuristic Function

The term 'heuristic' is a theory in education based on the idea that a learner should discover things himself. The heuristic function of language refers to language as a means of investigating reality, a way of learning about things that are using language to learn and to discover. It is the use of language for inquiry or questioning.

f. The Imaginative Function

'To imagine' means to form a picture of something in the mind, think of the probability of things. The imaginative function of language refers to the language used to create a world of the 15 imagination. It is the use of language for its own sake to give pleasure imaginatively and aesthetically. For example: "If I was an apple and grew on a tree I think I'd drop down on a nice boy like me; I wouldn't stay there, giving nobody joy, I'd fall down at once and say, Eat me, my boy!" - Anonymous

g. The Representational Function

'To represent' means to depict, show, describe or present in words. The representational function of language refers to the language used to communicate information. It is the use of language to convey a message which has specific reference to the processes, persons, objects, qualities, states and relations of the real world around us. For ex: books, newspapers, magazines, novels, use of language in mass media, etc.

Principles of Language Learning

Children can learn any language as easily as by walking, running, playing, etc. People generally assume that those who study in English medium schools are good at English and those who study in government schools are poor in English. Language learning has little to do with the medium of school. It rather depends on teachers' application of principles of language learning. Let us see the principles of language learning.

a. Habit Formation

Language learning is a habit formation process. It is a process during which various language habits are formed. Therefore, listening, speaking, reading and writing habits are to be formed consciously and unconsciously.

b. Practice and Drill

Language learning is a habit-forming process. For this purpose, sufficient practice and drill are needed.

c. Oral Approach

A child learns to speak his mother tongue before reading or writing it. This principle should be adopted in learning and teaching a second or a foreign language.

d. Natural Order of Learning

Listening-Speaking-Reading-Writing (LSRW) is the natural order of learning a language. In this order, a child learns his or her mother tongue without any formal instruction. So this natural order of learning should be considered while teaching English.

e. Multi-Skill Approach

All four language skills are to be given their due importance when learning or teaching them. No skill should be overemphasized or neglected.

f. Selection and Gradation

One should proceed from simple to difficult in language learning; therefore, vocabulary and structures of language should be selected and graded as per their frequency, teachability and difficulty level.

g. Situational Approach

The English language should be taught in situations which is the natural way in which a child learns his mother tongue.

h. Exposure

A child learns his mother tongue because he is exposed to it. While learning a foreign language like English, exposure to it helps in learning it.

i. Imitation

The child learns his mother tongue by imitation. The English teacher must provide a good model of speech for the learners. Audio-visual aids should be used.

j. Motivation

Motivation plays an important role in learning a language. Thus, learners should be motivated.

k. Accuracy

The English teacher should insist on accuracy in all aspects of language learning. So learners follow their teachers and consider them as role models.

l. Purpose

The purpose of language learning should be decided in the beginning. So it becomes a simple affair to design a course suitable for the purpose.

m. Multiple Approaches

The English teacher should not stick to a particular method of teaching. He should use all methods, approaches and techniques of teaching English as per the needs and requirements of learners.

n. Interest

The teacher should generate a great deal of energy and interest among learners so they will pay attention to learning a language.

o. Co-relation

If teaching-learning of English is co-related with real life then learners will realize the need for language learning and will take interest in it.

Nature of English Language

English is a varied language that has absorbed vocabulary from many languages of the world. English is the most dynamic language in the world. Let us discuss the nature of the English language.

a. Receptive

Receptiveness is regarded as an extraordinary nature of the English language. It has maintained its open-door policy. It has adopted and accepted thousands of words from European, Asian, African, Indian, Japanese, Chinese and other languages. We can see a great impact on classical languages like Latin, Greek, Arabic, French and Sanskrit on English. English has the richest vocabulary due to its receptiveness.

b. Heterogeneous

As English contains vocabulary from many languages, it has become heterogeneous in nature. In the process of adopting words from other languages, in some cases the original words as it is without change in meaning, but in some other cases, the spelling, pronunciation and meaning of original words from other languages were changed for instance; the French word, 'tour' and the Latin word, 'turris' become 'Tower' in English.

c. Systematic

The system of the English language functions through sounds, words and structures. The system of sound is known as phonology. The system of words is called morphology whereas the system of structures is named syntax. All these three systems are integrated with one another making an organic whole which is called the

English language.

d. Unique

English is unique in its nature. English is not 100% French, not German or Arabic, not Latin or Greek. English is English. English differs from other languages in its sounds, words, structures and functioning. Though English has adopted vocabulary from other languages, it has shaped them remarkably as if these words are their own.

e. Dynamic

English is a dynamic language. It is constantly changing. These changes are regular and systematic. If you study the history of the English language, you will come to know the difference between Old English, Medieval English and Modern English. The old English words like; 'thou and thee' are now 'you and your.' In the age of technology, we have developed 'SMS English' where many short forms are used such as; 'you' is written as 'u', 'as soon as possible' is written as 'ASAP', and 'your' is written as 'ur'. Our Bollywood stars mix Hindi with English, hence a new language comes into existence, which is 'Hinglish', where some sentences are spoken in English and some in Hindi. Sometimes, half of the sentence is spoken in Hindi and the other half is in English. So English is a dynamic language, therefore, it is continuously changing throughout the world.

f. Creative

English is a highly creative language, that's why it has the richest literature in the world. A writer or speaker can write or speak something he has never written or said before. English literature has a wide variety of prose and poetry, fiction and non-fictional writing, such as; 19 novels, short stories, travelogues, fairy tales, science fiction, drama, songs, etc. Because of the creative power of English, English literature is very easy to listen to and read.

g. Productive

English is also highly productive. One can make thousands and lakhs of sentences with its words. There is no need to learn by rote English sentences. We can produce sentences without effort. People speak and write in different ways and styles best still, the words and sentence structures are the same. The world is rapidly producing knowledge with the help of English which is doubling every 13 months. h. Symbolic English is symbolic. Every English word, phrase or sentence represents some object, activity or idea. For ex; after listening to the sentence, 'Sami was singing a song.' we can visualize how Sami could be singing the song. The announcement, 'The Ajanta Express is arriving on platform no 1,' creates a mental picture of the train arriving on a particular platform. So, English is symbolic in its nature.

i. Modifiable

English is extremely modifiable. It penetrates, fuses and assimilates with the local language of a given country to emerge in different modified and extended forms of English to be accepted, understood and enjoyed universally, such as; Indian English, American English, British English, Australian English, etc.

j. Grammatical

English has its own grammatical rules and structures of sentences. These grammatical rules and sentence structures are necessary for the proper relationship of the words in a sentence and to avoid ambiguity. It also clarifies the acceptable and unacceptable forms of sentences. For example; 'I am writing a book' is the correct order of present continuous tense rather than the sentence 'I book writing.' Therefore, Functional English grammar is essential for learning the English language.

Aims of Teaching English

Let us try to understand what are the aims of teaching English? It can be summarized as under

a. **General Aim**

The general aim of teaching English is to make the learner an effective user of the English language.

a. **Cultural Aim**

The cultural aim of teaching English is to enable the learners to know all the cultural groups of the world in general and cultural groups of India in particular. It will help in exchanging cultural values and eradicating cultural evils; such as superstitions, ignorance, untouchability, intolerance, extremism, etc and a rich and tolerant multi-cultural society can be established.

c. **Literary Aim**

The literary aim of teaching English is to open the treasure of rich English literature for Indians, such as; poetry, drama, prose works and fiction and enable them to produce Indian English literature to communicate the Indian philosophy, culture, values and dynamics to the world.

d. **Utilitarian Aim**

The utilitarian aim of teaching English is to open the gates of opportunities in different fields of life, education, travel, science, technology and international affairs.

e. **Linguistic Aim**

The linguistic aim of teaching English is to enable the learners to understand the system of English words (Morphology), sounds (Phonology) and sentences (Syntax).

f. **Integrative Aim**

The integrative aim of teaching English is to inculcate the integrative quality of the English language that unites people all across the world and India.

General Objectives of Teaching English

The general objectives of teaching and learning the English language can be summarized as follows:

i. **Listening**

It enables the learners to:

a. listen to English sounds properly;
b. listen to words with meaning expressed by others;
c. give the response to the talk of the teacher;
d. recognize and tell the meaning of the words and sentences expressed by the teacher;
e. reproduce whatever he has listened from the teacher; and
f. Organize the ideas listened to.

ii. **Speaking**

It enables the learners to:

a. use the proper pronunciation in speaking English.
b. use correct stress and intonation in speaking English.
c. speak grammatically correct.
d. tell the answers to the questions asked by the teacher.
e. take part in debate and conversation.
f. use appropriate vocabulary while speaking English.
g. speak English fluently.

iii. **Reading**

It enables the learners to:

a. read English letters, words and sentences correctly and properly.
b. tell the meaning of the words and sentences provided in the written form.
c. read English with proper stress, intonation, and pronunciation.
d. read lessons loudly and silently.
e. read English with proper pauses.

iv. **Writing**

It enables the learners to:

a. write English letters, words and sentences correctly.
b. use capital and small letters in the proper places.
c. use proper punctuation marks.
d. write answers correctly.
e. write a composition on a simple topic.
f. express the thoughts and ideas in a written form.
g. write grammatically correct.
h. write English with proper speed.

Objectives of Teaching English at Different Levels of Education

Objectives of teaching English at different levels of education, primary and secondary levels are as under;

a. **Primary Level**

At the primary level learner should:

1. understand English when spoken;
2. acquire the reading ability and read the material that is appropriate for his level;
3. acquire a vocabulary enough to help him in the use of the language that he makes;
4. make simple statements in English;
5. speak with a pronunciation that is acceptable;
6. respond to short conversational questions and ask questions himself;
7. write English legibly and coherently using proper punctuation and spelling; and
8. use English when he has to respond to calls, requests, greetings, etc. when he has to do the same to others.

b. **Secondary Level**

At the secondary level the learner should:

1. speak English fluently and accurately;
2. speak freely. They should think in English and speak it with ease and frequently;
3. express their ideas in English in the classroom at school, at home and in society;

4. respond and react to situations actively and not remain only a passive listener;
5. acquire the ability to understand the native speakers and also be able to respond to them;
6. compose freely and independently in speech and writing;
7. read books, newspapers and periodicals with understanding;
8. develop sufficient command over vocabulary that should include frequent and choicest English phrases and idioms; and
9. use reference material like encyclopedias, dictionaries, reference books, etc.

Objectives of Teaching English Related to Language Forms

The following are some of the curricular objectives related to prose and poetry lessons listed by

M. Jesa (2005) in his book, '*Efficient English Teaching*';

a. **Prose**

The teacher enables the learner to:

a. listen to short speeches, narratives, and commentaries;
b. take notes on the listened piece of prose;
c. enjoy puzzles and riddles; express ideas in one's own way;
d. take part in seminars, and discussions;
e. present piece of dialogue;
f. dramatize situations;

g. express ideas selecting the appropriate words and functions;
h. read and understand short essays;
a. understand messages, advertisements, brochures;
j. compile dictionary in a simple form;
k. sequence ideas and present in writing;
ax. suggest appropriate title;
all. expand an idea;
n. write letters using different formats;
o. write dialogue and reviews; and
p. prepare reports and brochures.

2. **Poetry**

The teacher enables learners to:

1. listen to and recite poems;
2. appreciate rhythm and feelings;
3. collect recordings of poems;
4. write a few poetic lines; and
5. collect poems with the same rhythmic pattern.

Status of English in the Global and Indian Context - Scope of English Language

English is an international language. English has been playing an important role in our educational system as well as in our national life. English was supreme in the pre-independent India, because of British rule over India. English still occupies an important place and position in courts, trade, commerce, industry, the educational system and the national life of India. Let us see the scope of English through the following points;

a. **An Official Language**

English was the official language of administration during the British period. After the independence of India, English has been declared the Associate Official Language of the Union of India for an indefinite period by an Act of Parliament in 1963. As such it dominates the administrative business at the centre as well as in the states. All the administrative work is done in English throughout the country.

b. **Language of Court**

English still continues to be the language of the courts. So far there is no other suitable language for legal business. Cases are presented and judgments are given in English in Supreme, High and District courts of India.

c. **Language of International Trade and Industry**

English dominates the fields of trade and industry in the country. Because all the work in these fields is carried on in English, such as; maintenance of accounts, audits and correspondence.

d. **A Link Language**

English is a national link language of India as well as an international link language of the world. It is the only language which is understood in all states of India and all countries of the world. We can establish social, economic, cultural and political relations with other countries and other states of India only through English.

e. **A Library Language**

English is the key to the storehouse of knowledge. Most of this knowledge is not yet available in Indian languages. It is in this context that the role of English as a library language becomes important in India.

f. **Importance in Education**

English plays an important role in the field of education. It is taught as a compulsory subject in most of the states in the country. It is the medium of instruction in technical, medical, law,

science, commerce and other institutions. A large number of English medium schools of SSC, CBSE, ICSE patterns are providing education through English as a medium of instruction.

g. **Window to the Modern World**

Pandit Nehru had rightly said, "English is our major window on the modern world." English is a window through which we can see the scientific, technological, agricultural and commercial developments taking place in the world. English is the only language through which we have distilled the essence of modern knowledge in all fields of human activity.

h. **Importance in Social Life**

English plays an important role in the social life of the country. The highly educated and sophisticated sections of our society find it more convenient to talk in English.

Invitation cards are mostly printed in English. People generally do signatures in English. People use thousands of English words in their day to day language. Bills in almost all the shops are in English.

i. **Lingua Franca of India and World**

Lingua Franca means the language of communication used by people belonging to different languages. English is the Lingua Franca of not only India but throughout the world.

j. **Language of Western Science and Arts**

English was the key which opened the gates of western sciences and arts to Indians. By learning English, they not only got a peep into the western sciences and arts but some of them also acquired mastery over them. For ex: scientists like Raman, philosophers like Radhakrishnan, poets like Tagore, etc.

k. **Language of Science and Technology**

English is the language of science and information & communication technology on which the management and administration of the entire world are dependent. Without English, we cannot learn modern science and information and communication technology.

ax. Language of our Literary Development

The credit for developing the Indian languages goes to English. By reading English books, Indian writers developed their own language and literature. The development of modern Indian novels, short stories, dramas and literary criticism is entirely due to the impact of English on Indian languages. Such are the reasons that helped English to become an important language in not only India but throughout the world.

Teaching English in Bilingual/Multilingual Contexts - Teaching English as a Second Language

According to Wikipedia (2017), 'A person's second language is a language that is not the native language of the speaker, but that is used in the locale of that person.' In other words, a second language is learned in addition to the mother tongue of the learner for its practical utility in day to day life and affairs. Therefore, the mother tongue of the learner is called the first language or L1 and any language that is learned in addition to the mother tongue is known as the second language or L2. Languages are also classified into many such types' i.e. third language (L3), foreign language, a dead language, classical language, target language, etc.

In the present context, English has acquired the place of the Second language in India for its national and global importance as a language of knowledge, communication, education, business, trade, commerce, science, technology and a window on the modern world. Therefore, English has been used by Indians for utilitarian purposes, such as; for social, commercial, official and educational activities within the country and abroad, for listening to the national and global broadcasts, reading newspapers and books and travelling across the country or world.

It is very important for a teacher of English to make his learners equipped with the command of English which allows him to express himself in speech or in writing that can sustain them in the present world which functions through the English language. Teachers should realize the objectives of teaching English as a second language and enable the learners to:

understand English when spoken;

a. speak English correctly and fluently;
b. read English with comprehension at a reasonable speed for gathering information and enjoy reading;
c. write English neatly and correctly with proper speed and legibility;
d. acquire knowledge of the elements of English for achieving a practical command of the language; and
e. translate English into their mother tongue and vice-versa.

Keeping in view the above objectives the teacher educators should design the syllabus of English and teachers should plan their teaching activities. If you observe the teaching of English in Indian classrooms, you will come across the following dull irrelevant activities of teachers, such as; writing new words on the blackboard with their mother tongue meanings, instructing learners to write them down in their notebooks, asking learners to memorize the words and their meanings by heart, reading aloud three to four passages of prose and translating it into their mother tongue, explaining some grammatical items and telling learners to write down the answers to the questions given at the end of the lesson as their homework, etc. Through such activities, we are not going to achieve the objectives of teaching English as a second language. Teachers should follow the principles of language learning.

Language and Educational Policy in India; Constitutional Provisions and policies of language education

Before the independence of India, English was an official language. It was the language of rulers, courts, banks, trade and industry, administration, link language between rulers and ruled and medium of instruction in schools, colleges and universities. So it occupied a privileged place in India. But with the attainment of Independence in 1947, the position of English in our education as well as in our national life came to be seriously questioned. Some national leaders supported English while some were committed to driving away English from India.

Many educationists and national leaders came to the conclusion that English should be replaced by one Indian language. But however, all of them were quite reluctant to drive away from English from India owing to its worldwide importance. C.Rajgopalcharya, M.Gandhi, Pandit Jawaharlal Nehru supported English. Some leaders were advocating the Hindi language to be adopted as the national and official language of India but it was seriously opposed by some states of south India.

India being a multilingual country was in need of a language policy because it was a sentimental issue for its people. The forefathers of this country wisely dealt with this issue through constitutional provisions and addressing the diverse language needs of the country. Let us know some of the constitutional provisions that define the language policy of India.

Article 343: Official language of the Union

1. The official language of the Union shall be Hindi in the Devanagari script. The form of numerals to be used

for the official purposes of the Union shall be the international form of Indian numerals.

2. Notwithstanding anything in clause (1), for a period of fifteen years from the commencement of this Constitution, the English language shall continue to be used for all the official purposes of the Union for which it was being used immediately before such commencement:

Provided that the President may, during the said period, by order authorise the use of the Hindi language in addition to the English language and of the Devanagari form of numerals in addition to the international form of Indian numerals for any of the official purposes of the Union.

Notwithstanding anything in this article, Parliament may by law provide for the use, after the said period of fifteen years, of

a. The English language, or
b. The Devanagari form of numerals, for such purposes as may be specified in the law.

Article 350A: Facilities for instruction in mother-tongue at the primary stage

It shall be the endeavour of every State and of every local authority within the State to provide adequate facilities for instruction in the mother tongue at the primary stage of education to children belonging to linguistic minority groups and the President may issue such directions to any State as he considers necessary or proper for securing the provision of such facilities.

Article 351: Directive for development of the Hindi language

It shall be the duty of the Union to promote the spread of the Hindi language, to develop it so that it may serve as a medium of expression for all the elements of the composite culture of India and to secure its enrichment by assimilating without interfering with its genius, the style and expressions of the form used in Hindustani and in the other languages of India specified in the Eighth Schedule, and by drawing, wherever necessary or desirable, for its vocabulary, primarily on Sanskrit and secondarily on other languages. All of the above articles or their sub-clauses clearly show that the country has given due importance to English, Hindi and all other regional languages concerning their international, national and regional importance respectively.

Kothari Commission (1964-66) precisely introduced a 'three language formula' that advocates:

a. The First language to be studied must be the mother tongue or the regional language.
b. The Second language – In Hindi speaking States, the second language will be some other modern Indian language or English, and in non-Hindi speaking States, the second language will be Hindi or English.
c. The Third language – In Hindi speaking States, the third language will be English or a modern Indian language not studied as the second language, and – In non-Hindi speaking States, the third language will be English or a modern Indian language not studied as the second language (Teaching of Indian Language, Position paper, NCERT, 2006.). But now in most of the states of India, English is taught as a compulsory subject from standard one to graduation. Today, Indian learners learn English as a second language.

The National Policy on Education (1986) and its revision, Programme of Action (1992) presented a detailed report regarding; the three-language formula, improvements in the linguistic competencies at the different stages of education, Provision of facilities for the study of English and other foreign languages, and Development of Hindi language as a link language. The policy emphasized the use of regional languages as a medium of instruction in higher education. The report mentioned the following:

"The energetic development of Indian Languages and literature is a sine qua non for educational and cultural development. Unless this is done, the creative energies of the people will not be released, standards of education will not improve, knowledge will not spread to the people and the gulf between the intelligentsia and masses will remain if not widen further. The regional languages are already in use as media of education at the primary and secondary stages. Urgent steps should now be taken to adopt them as media of education at the university stage."(National Policy on Education (With Modifications Undertaken In 1992, 39)

The POA (1992) in chapter 18, 'Developing Languages (page no 94 – 98),' observed that the implementation of the three-language formula had been less than satisfactory on account of;

a. All the languages are not being taught compulsorily at the secondary stage
b. A classical language has been substituted for a modern Indian language in some States
c. No concrete provision yet exists (though a scheme is likely to take off very soon) for the teaching of South Indian languages in the Hindi speaking states

d. Duration for the compulsory study of three languages varies and
e. Competency levels to be achieved by learners of each language have not been precisely specified.

POA (1992) suggested the following recommendations for the effective implementation of the Three Language Formula:

a. Decision by States, State Boards of Secondary/schools education, etc., to make the study of three languages compulsory at the secondary stage;
b. Prescription of the class from and the duration for which three languages will be taught;
c. Specification of objectives of teaching different languages. The State Boards of Secondary Education will be asked to take uniform decisions in line with the recommendations of NCERT and CBSE in these matters; and
d. Specification of levels of language proficiency to be reached in respect of each language. Language institutions under the Ministry like Kendriya Hindi Sansthan (KHS), Central Institute of Indian Languages (CIIL), and Central Institute of English and Foreign Languages (CIEFL) in consultation with NCERT would be asked to prescribe minimum competencies to be achieved.

POA (1992) also suggested a plan of action to implement the above recommendations. After POA (1992), the most noteworthy recommendations were given by National Curriculum Framework (2005).

The policy suggested promoting Hindi as a link language in the following recommendation:

"Every effort should be made to promote the development of Hindi. In developing Hindi as the link language, due care should be taken to ensure that it will serve, as provided for in Article 351 of the Constitution, as a medium of expression for all the elements of the composite culture of India. The establishment, in non-Hindi States, of colleges and other institutions of higher education which use Hindi, as the medium of education should be encouraged."(National Policy on Education (With Modifications Undertaken In 1992), page no. 40)

Another noteworthy language policy can be seen in National Curriculum Framework (2005). National Curriculum Framework (2005) in its third chapter, 'Curricular Areas, School Stages and Assessment, page no; 36-37' sheds light on language education in the country and suggested following guidelines:

- Language teaching needs to be multilingual not only in terms of the number of languages offered to children but also in terms of evolving strategies that would use the multilingual classroom as a resource.
- Home language(s) of children should be the medium of learning in schools.
- If a school does not have provisions for teaching in the child's home language(s) at the higher levels, primary school education must still be covered by the home language(s). It is imperative that we honour the child's home language(s). According to Article 350A of our Constitution, 'It shall be the endeavour of every State and of every local authority within the State to provide adequate facilities for instruction in the mother-tongue

at the primary stage of education to children belonging to linguistic minority groups'.

- Children will receive multilingual education from the outset. The three-language formula needs to be implemented in its spirit, promoting multilingual communicative abilities for a multilingual country.
- In the non-Hindi-speaking states, children learn Hindi. In the case of Hindi speaking states, children learn a language not spoken in their area. Sanskrit may also be studied as a Modern Indian Language (MIL) in addition to these languages.
- At later stages, the study of classical and foreign languages may be introduced.

Home language means mother tongue of children. NCF (2005) asserted the importance of multilingualism and mentioned that "Multilingualism, which is constitutive of the identity of a child and a typical feature of the Indian linguistic landscape, must be used as a resource, classroom strategy and a goal by a creative language teacher. This is not only the best use of a resource readily available but also a way of ensuring that every child feels secure and accepted and that no one is left behind on account of his/ her linguistic background (NCF(2005), p. 36)."

In this way, we have taken a short account of language policy of our country.

CHAPTER III

FANTASIES OF A MAKE BELIEF WORLD: AN ANALYSIS ON THE INFLUENCE OF CARTOONS, A VISUAL MEDIUM ON CHILDREN

Joshna Francis
Assistant Professor, Dept. of English,
Bhavan's College of Arts & Commerce, Kakkanad

ABSTRACT

This article examines the impact of visual culture on children through cartoons. In our society, children are very much interested in watching cartoons and shows on Television. The new generation has no life without the small screen. Cartoons, a unique visual medium, claiming to be neither a reality nor art, have become reality for our children who are growing up in front of it. It is one of the favourite programs of children and has become a part of their daily routine. It is integral and natural to their being. The purpose of this study is to investigate the pervasiveness of cartoons in the lives of children.

A strong visual tool like a cartoon can be described as a double-edged weapon since it has got both positive and negative effects. On a positive note, it can be said that cartoons give information about different people and cultures. It teaches helping, sharing and empathy and also supports literary skills. It helps children obtain knowledge about events and objects that they may not experience in daily life. Over the decades, cartoons have changed drastically but have their influence on children. A child watching too many cartoons on T.V. is more likely to have mental and psychological issues. The cartoons through the messages, heroes' action or dialogue affect the child's attitude and thereby, creates a make-belief world around the child. Do the children gain positively or negatively from the viewing of the cartoons? The text tries to untangle this question.

Keywords: Cartoons, visual media, children, visual literacy and behaviour

INTRODUCTION

Communicating views, thoughts, ideas or information through visuals can be termed visual communication. This is done effectively with the help of visual media, a means of visual culture. Visual media gives prime importance to what humans perceive. It has a significant role in advertising, art, communication, education, business and engineering. Forms of visual media comprise digital and printed images, photography, graphic design, fashion, videos, architectural structures and fine arts. Cartoons can be considered one of the visual media since it depends on visual guidelines and is appealing to the visual senses.

A person who creates cartoons is known as a cartoonist. The cartoon is a visual art represented in the form of drawings or paintings which is meant to depict humour, satire or caricature. It has been a part of the film field since the first motion pictures were made in the late 1800s. A cartoon is a moving picture made by using animatronics instead of living performers, particularly a hilarious portrayal envisioned for children. It is an upcoming genre in the area of environment. Cartoons communicate with the help of body language of characters, gestures, facial expressions, verbal communication, voice modulation, setting or the background of the pictures, stereotypes and caricatures, words used by the characters (speech bubbles), and thoughts of the characters (thought bubbles), the scale of each character in relation to the another (importance and presentation of the cartoon characters), colours used in the cartoon, the environment in which the character is set, the overall presentation of the characters, the plot, the typical features portrayed by the characters, the conversations, in-between dialogues of the characters, the actions. Cartoons make the maximum use of visuals which results in successful visual communication.

Fantasies of a Make Belief World: An Analysis on the Influence of Cartoons, a Visual Medium on Children.

Origin of Cartoons

The concept of cartoons originated in Middle Ages. It was first used to define a preparatory drawing for a piece of art, such as a painting, fresco, tapestry, or stained glass window. In the 19thcentury, it came to refer to simple drawings showing the features of its subjects in a humorously exaggerated way, especially a satirical one in a newspaper or magazine. After the early 20th century, it was denoted as comic strips and animated films. An animated cartoon is a film for the cinema, television or computer screen, which is made using sequential drawings, as opposed to animations in general, which include films made using clay, puppet and other means. Because of the aesthetic resemblances between comic strips and early animated movies, cartoons came to refer to as animation and the term "cartoon" is currently used in reference to both animated cartoons and gag cartoons. A Gag cartoon, is most often a single-panel cartoon, usually including a caption beneath the drawing. A pantomime cartoon carries no caption. In some cases, dialogue may appear in speech balloons, following the common convention of comic strips. While animation designates any style of illustrated images seen in rapid succession to give the impression of movement, the word "cartoon" is most often used as a descriptor for television programs and short films aimed at children, possibly featuring anthropomorphized animals, superheroes adventures of child protagonists and/or related themes.

Cartoons and Children

What do our children watch generally on television? It is cartoons. Children are the craziest followers of cartoons. Today, it has become a part of their daily life. They love to spend the whole day simply watching their favourite cartoon characters. They will not even hesitate or rethink, before replacing their much-loved outdoor games and glue themselves to the television in order to follow their regular cartoons. More and more parents put their little children in front of the television to keep them out of trouble. Children would sit for hours watching cartoons and get amused by their content. Here, the cartoon plays the role of a babysitter.

For children, the cartoon is a companion which helps them to eradicate their monotony. Children are wooed by the cartoon characters which represent humour, fun and adventure. And that's why they are attracted to it. Children get easily attached to cartoons as they can relate themselves to these animated figures and the surroundings or the circumstances to which they belong. They feel that they are one among those creatures. Children enjoy cartoons not only because it is entertaining but also are relaxing as well. It gives them pleasure by taking them to a different world – a stress-free world. It leads children to another realm which is devoid of any kind of tension. It gives the impression that life's problems can be settled in a matter of minutes.

Actually, children are trapped under the illusion of cartoon channels.

Children do not go out of the house and experience real life or interact with others. They do not understand the complexities of life. They do not learn to handle them. They grow up believing that they can control the world. When they go to school they come to realize that life is much more complex and difficult than what they were made to believe. Then only they will come out of their dreamland and realize that cartoons are merely visual representations of non-realistic or semi-realistic events and that it has not got any power to solve the problems of life magically. The booming of cartoon film in a television programs has become a very complicated matter. It has been a long-standing concern for both parents as well as educationalists. However, cartoon influences the lives of children both positively and negatively.

Positive Effects

There are many advantages to watching cartoons. With good guidance and proper limitations, cartoons could be beneficial to kids. Early childhood is the golden age of new skills. The child learns to act and behave by imitating others. The child develops a variety of motor skills. Perceptual development begins from mass movements to differentiation and integration. The unique characterization of cartoons helps the child to remember and to distinguish each character. Cartoons teach effective problem-solving. For instance, take the cartoon Bob, the Builder. In this particular show, Bob the Builder and his construction crew face building, renovation, and repair challenges. The series often focuses on identifying a problem and making a plan to solve the problem.

Cartoon gives information about different people and cultures. This can be seen in the cartoon Chhota Bheem. The character Chhota Bheem is the namesake of a very popular character in mythology called Bheemand is known for his eating habits and huge strength. The story of Chhota Bheem revolves around his bravery and win of good over evil and is set in a village within a very cosy environment with his friends. The children can relate to these in their own environment which is why the series is a hit with them. Also, the characters portray Indian cultures and traditions like Mela or festivals like Raksha Bandhan, Holi, Diwali and so on. Friendship is highly valued and evil is destroyed in the end restoring faith in the good. Each episode teaches some moral values but with a tinge of entertainment, fun and humour, which makes the programme and the character all the more lovable. It teaches helping, sharing and empathy.

Good home environment and early childhood practice help in the development of vocabulary. The intellectual development of the child is accelerated because now he begins to explore his social environment and acquires new experiences. By the age of six, the child develops the perception of size, shape, colour, etc. Memory increases during the early childhood period. By this time the child is able to use symbols in language. Early childhood is a critical period in the development of speech skills as future habits are influenced by these skills. The ability to understand meaning develops during this period and the instinct of curiosity is very high.

Through cartoons, kids are able to learn new vocabulary hence improving their speech and use of vocabulary in writing which is of great benefit in education. In one of the famous cartoons, Dora the Explorer, the main lead Dora is a bilingual Latin girl. Dora and her friends go on quests and help others, encouraging viewers to help out through their own actions or by telling her what she needs to know. In addition to highlighting traditional educational content such as colour and shapes, Dora teaches language by repeating words and phrases in English and Spanish. Cartoons enhance literary skills and support learning by presenting issues about real life.

The content of cartoons is age and developmentally appropriate. There are even programs which target toddlers. It helps them to differentiate each colour and obtain knowledge about events and objects that they may not experience in daily life. It helps children to obtain knowledge about new areas of interest. By watching cartoon films, children become more creative. They try to do things in different ways. So their imagination and creativity are enhanced. There is also evidence in the literature that children's imaginative play can be positively affected by television content . The children get new ideas with which they can show their talent.

Visual literacy can be attained through cartoon characters. When John Debes, the founder of the international visual literacy society (IVLA), coined the term in 1969, he proposed the following definition:

Visual literacy refers to a group of vision competencies a human being can develop by seeing and at the same time having and integrating other sensory experiences. The development of these competencies is fundamental to normal human learning. When developed, they enable a visually literate person to discriminate and interpret the visible actions, objects, and symbols, natural or man-made, that he encounters in his environment. Through the creative use of these, he is able to communicate with others. Through the appreciative use of these competencies, he is able to comprehend and enjoy the masterworks of visual communication" (Ganwer 2). Ganwer also felt that a person "becomes visually literate by the practice of visual encoding (expressing thoughts and ideas in visual form) and visual decoding (translating the content and meaning of visual imagery), (Ganwer, 3).

Visual literacy has been defined as the "ability to understand, interpret and evaluate visual messages" (Bristor and Drake 74). Cartoons communicate in a variety of ways resulting in successful visual communication and thereby, helping children to boost their concentration and achieve visual literacy. Besides these advantages, a cartoon is a good form of entertainment. The children are better to see cartoons than seeing other television programs like crime news, electron cinema, unethical show, etc. Cartoons give kids safe satisfying entertainment rather than them watching other forms which might be violent.

Negative Effects

Children watching too many cartoons are likely to have mental, emotional and psychological problems. It may even lead to physical problems by hurting their eyesight. It impacts the way children play. Cartoon viewing has replaced outdoor games that were initially important in the growth of children. It has substituted physical exercise. Cartoons have influenced children so much that they can be seen in their choice of toys. Children are very much addicted to cartoons. It reduces children's communication with their family members or adults. They want to watch, they don't want to be spoken to or talked to or singled out...So they grow up essentially mute...Instead of coming of age, they're growing apart.

Children enjoy the fantasies of the make-belief world that cartoon creates around them. Cartoon diverts children from real life. Because in most cartoons problems are solved in unrealistic ways or by using the power which is irrational and illogical. It includes imaginary contents. When children recognize that they were breathing in a visual cultural atmosphere constructed by their favourite cartoons, it will create mistrust in children. This will make them frustrated. They may become demanding, impatient and violent. They feel persecuted. In other words, cartoon hampers the healthy growth of children's minds.

Cartoon exhibits biases towards occupations and towards people with disabilities or people who look different. This may lead the child to have a judgemental personality. The cartoon contains negative emotions, such as fear and aggressiveness. Children can learn aggressive behaviour through observation. Albert Bandura believes children observe and learn aggression through many avenues, but the three main principles are family, communities and media. According to Bandura, "Modeling is the basis of observational learning" (87). By observing the behaviour of others or models, individuals repeat the behaviour. Punishment of bad cartoon characters encourages the idea of violence in children. They will become less sensitive to the pain and sufferings of others. While violent content influences children's behaviour, content that doesn't include violent scenes with low-quality educational value may also negatively impact children's attention and cognition.

CONCLUSION

The first and most important effect of watching cartoons in children is its modifying effect on the behaviour of children. This article shows that cartoons help to form good character as well as modify the wrong character in children, especially in modern times. Cartoons can also influence the attitude of children negatively. Cartoon as a visual medium is here to stay. The danger is in the use we make of it. Cartoon producers and parents can take steps to maximize the positive effects of this visual device and minimize the negative effects. The negative effects through strict monitoring from parents may easily turn around to positivity. Parents can select well-designed, age-appropriate programs and view the programs with their children to maximize the positive effects. This will help the children to continue gaining the benefits of cartoons.

WORKS CITED

Baker, R. K. and S .J. Ball. *Mass media and violence: A staff report to the National Commission on the Causes and Prevention of Violence*, 9. U. S. Government Printing Office, 1969.

Bandura, Albert. *Social learning theory*. Englewood Cliffs, NJ: Prentice-Hall, 1997.

Bristor, V.J. and S.V. Drake. *Linking the Language Arts and Content Areas through Visual Technology*. Cornell UP, 1994.

Ganwer, T. *Visual impact, visual teaching*.2nd ed. Thousand Oaks, CA: Corwin Press, 2009.

Mirzoeff, Nicholas. *An Introduction to Visual Culture.* Routledge,1999.

Thankachan.T.C and Jose P. Mattam. *Educational Psychology: Concepts and Theories*, 2009.

BIO-NOTE

Ms. Joshna Francis holds a Master's in English from St. Albert's College, Ernakulam and resides in Fort Kochi. She has completed her B.Ed. in English and has qualified SET. She is in the 6th year of her teaching career. She joined Bhavan's College of Arts & Commerce, as an Assistant Professor on contract in the Department of English in 2016.

CHAPTER IV

THE FEMINIST RELOOKING OF KAVITHA KANE IN FICTIONALISING RAMAYANA AND MAHABHARATA

Meera K. S.

Assistant Professor, Department of English

Sree Mahadeva College, Vaikom, Kottayam.

ABSTRACT

This paper is a sincere attempt to investigate the works of Indian English writer Kavitha Kane in the light of feminism. The main aim is an introspection into the Great Indian Epics Ramayana and Mahabharatha. The selected works of Kane are based on the marginalised female characters in these epics. This article relates the idea of marginalisation and feminism in a single line.

Our *epics* and Puranas are a source of endless inspiration for writers, filmmakers, and artists and the multitude of characters and threads take myriad shapes and directions in their able hands. The *retelling* of our *epics* is not new in fact, it is said that the *Ramayana* has 300 versions. *Mahabharata* is the largest epic in the world and may have versions more than that. There is a saying about *Mahabharata* that what it contains is everywhere in the world and what does is nowhere exists. Kavitha Kane is one of the versatile geniuses in recreating mythological stories into new versions like *Karna's Wife, Sita's Sister, Lanka's Princess' Menaka's Choice* and *The Fisher Queen's Dynasty.*

Kavitha Kane is popularly known for bringing to attention the marginalised woman characters in mythology.

Her novels are women-centric, especially the lesser-known women in mythology. *Sita's Sister* is her second novel which depicts the life of Sita's younger sister Urmila, the future wife of Laxmana. Going back to how she began writing, much before her first book Karna's Wife gave her a cult following, Kane was a journalist who had 'not handled creative writing, not even in a college magazine. Her fondness for mythology was cultivated in childhood by a staple diet of *Amar Chitra Katha books, Ramayana and Mahabharata.*

Barring a few exceptions, women find scant mentions in epics like Ramayana and Mahabharata and her work carries a necessary trend of resuscitating the tales of marginalised female characters from these epics. Her novels are women-centric, about relatively lesser-known women in mythology and depict issues and problems of women relevant even in the modern era. Here is a list of her works, all of which are feminist retellings of Indian mythology.

Kane's second novel, *Sita's Sister* is part reality rendition of Ramayan from the perspective of Urmila, Sita's younger sister and the wife of Lakshman. It is essentially a book that talks about all the women in Ramayana but Urmila comes out as the most influential character, who is headstrong yet calm in the face of adversity and can look at the bigger picture. She comes across as an individual who accepted her situations gracefully, whether it is by being second fiddle to the adopted elder sister Sita or submitting to the fact that her husband would remain committed to his brotherly duties over and above her. Instead of lamenting, she reciprocates by being a source of strength for her loved ones. She is one of the strongest characters in Valmiki's Ramayana.

Her debut novel *Karna's Wife: The Outcast's Queen* is a poignant retelling of the epic Mahabharata from the eyes of a lesser-known character Uruvi, the second wife of Karna. The tale explores the multiple facets of Karna, the epitome of moral righteousness, who made all the wrong decisions in life owing to his loyalty to Duryodhana. Uruvi fails to forgive Karna for his transgression after the game of dice in ordering the disrobing of Draupadi. She is portrayed as a headstrong woman as a wife, trying to steer her husband clear of the evil Duryodhan and Shakuni, and as a mother, bringing up her child single-handedly and renouncing the throne of Hastinapur.

Menaka's choice chronicles the life of the most beautiful apsara in heaven, Menaka. The book is a re-telling of Menaka's trials and tribulations in her voice. After being constantly demeaned and reduced to the role of seductress, she refuses to be subdued and finally fights for her rights and honour. Menaka demands to be seen as a woman, to be granted the same rights as 'devis' and not be seen as mere entertainers in Indra's court. The book ends with an ultimate statement of empowerment where Menaka reasserts her right to choose.

The novel '*The Fisher Queen's Dynasty*' is the story of Mahabharata from Satyavati's perspective, the wife of King Shantanu and the step-mother of Bhishma Pitamah. The book explores human contradictions, between sticking to morals and rising on the social ladder through deceit through the character of the Satyavati, a fisher-girl who went on to become a queen. Abandoned as a baby, preyed on by a rishi, Satyavati rose in the station to become a queen and the grand matriarch of the Kuru dynasty. The trajectory of the story moves in line with the rise and fall of Satyavati's fortunes and Bhishm's sense of idealism. The book sets a daunting example of how one's decisions and actions can bring consequences in somebody's life, who is entirely disconnected from their life.

Through *Lanka's Princess*, Kane tells the story from the vantage of Surpanakha, Ravana's infamous sister, as more hated than hateful. Surpanakha is commonly perceived as ugly and untamed, brutal and brazen. One whose nose was sliced off by an angry Lakshman and the woman behind war but was she a perpetrator or a mere victim is what the book is all about. It unfolds the life of Meenakshi, aka Surpanakha, growing up like a neglected child overshadowed by her brothers, again facing a life of rejection.

For now, Kane is among the few, if not the only, persons doing that. As a striking example, she adds, We are more familiar with Kalidas' Shakuntala than the Shakuntala of the original text. The very nature of Kane's writings makes it inevitable that people will have issues with the content of her books. She is, after all, altering the existing, accepted version of mythology. She admits that readers often ask her probing questions, and she reckons it to be a good thing.

As I always say, mythology should make you think, not judge. she says.

Surpanakha or Lanka's Princess is an important character in Ramayana. Ravan's sister and the daughter of Vishravas, the grandson of Brahma, She is half Asura and half Rishi kanya. Like her siblings Raavan, Kumbhakarna and Vibhishan she is depicted to be more comfortable with her Asura bloodline than the other. Born as "Meenakshi" Surpanakha is renamed so because she has nails that are akin to sharp claws which she often uses for self-defence. In most Ramayana narratives, Surpanakha appears in the tenth year of Ram, Lakshman and Sita's exile. Their paths cross in the Dandak forest, where she resides along with her cousin Khara and Uncle Mareecha who are guarding the forest for their king, Raavan. In Valmiki's Ramayana, Surpanakha is depicted as an ugly Rakshashi who is driven mad with lust when she chances upon Ram in the Dandak forest. She appears before Ram and Lakshman and attempts to seduce Ram.

Ram and Lakshman are amused by her behaviour. Ram, catching the humour in the situation, dissuades her suggestive attempts and directs her toward Lakshman. Lakshman, who is also amused by a lady who is openly approaching men, directs her back to Ram. For a few minutes, they indulge in some fun at the cost of Surpanakha who is incensed when the realization strikes. Surpanakha aims to strike Sita and punish the two men for her humiliation but realizing her intention, Ram and Lakshman capture her and Ram orders Lakshman to punish her by maiming her. Lakshman then chops off her ears and nose to remind her of the fateful day for the rest of her life.

Saraswathi's Gift is another book about the Goddess Sarasvati. She is the Goddess of music, art, and knowledge. This book explains her creator Brahma and her unusual marriage with him. After reading, the reader will know how powerful the Goddess is and how important her story is buried under the myths. *Ahalya's Awakening* says the story of Ahalya who was created by Brahma; she was married to one of the greatest Rishis and was liked by Lord Indra. She was cursed. She got uncursed by Lord Rama.

She had more fascination for the more complex, even if secondary, characters in these books than the protagonists. And she gleaned an important insight from these books which was to shape her writings to come. Kane's own words show:

I always believed that mythology can be a huge canvas for contemporary thought. It is not telling us some old tales, as so carelessly assumed, of Gods and Goddesses, but of Man and his follies and fallacies.

How did Karna's wife react to her husband's role at Draupadi's 'vastraharan (disrobing) ?' Why is Surpanakha so widely censured? The more Kane read, the more consumed she became by such questions that even her grandmother could not satisfactorily answer. And thus she set about answering these questions herself. What Kane's writings do, very clearly, is to show readers that even mythology has become a victim of patriarchy. She says, If women have not been portrayed in a proper light, it's because of misogyny and chauvinism which made us all myopic and did not allow us to see these women for their enormous strength and conviction.

WORKS CITED

Kane, Kavitha. "Through the Mythical Lens".Interview by R. Karthika.The Hindu. 5th March 2020

Kane, Kavitha. *Karna's Wife: The Outcaste's Queen*. New Delhi: Rupa Publications Pvt. Ltd. 2013

Kane, Kavitha. *Sita's Sister*. New Delhi: Rupa Publications Pvt. Ltd. 2014

Kane, Kavitha. *Menaka's Choice*. New Delhi: Rupa Publications Pvt. Ltd. 2015

Kane, Kavitha. *Lanka's Princess* . New Delhi: Rupa Publications Pvt. Ltd. 2016

Kane, Kavitha. *The Fisher Queen's Dynasty*. New Delhi: Rupa Publications Pvt. Ltd. 2017

Kane, Kavitha. *Ahalya's Awakening*. New Delhi: Rupa Publications Pvt. Ltd. 2019

Kane, Kavitha. *Saraswati's Gift*. New Delhi: Rupa Publications Pvt. Ltd. 2021.

BIO- NOTE

Meera K. S. is an academician who had completed her Post Graduation from Devamatha College, Kuravilangad. She took her B.Ed from St. Mary's College, Karikode. She is a former Guest Lecturer in the BPC College, Piravom and St. Mary's Training College, Karikode. She had cleared UGC NET. She is an Assistant Professor at Sree Mahadeva College, Vaikom. She has published articles in international journals such as IJCRT, IJRAR, PIJR. She also published a chapter in an ISBN book ***Optima Scripta, Literarum Carmina, Indian English Poetry: A Critical Evaluation.*** She has presented research papers in the national conference conducted by Kristu Jayanti College, Bengaluru and in the international conference conducted by NIT, Agartala.

CHAPTER V

ADJUNCTION OF ACTOR NETWORK THEORY AND SCIENCE FICTION IN POSTHUMANISM.

Sali S.
Assistant Professor
Post-Graduate Department of English
Don Bosco Colleg, Kottiyam, Kerala

ABSTRACT

Posthumanism intends any theory that is critical of traditional humanism, ideas about humanity and the human condition. The concept of past humanism becomes a mode of philosophy, ethics and exposition that neglects the classic human divisions of self and the other, mind and body, society and nature, human and animal, organic and technological. This paper focuses on posthumanism Sci-Fi (Science Fiction) and Actor-Network-Theory. The actor is the source of action, and Actor-Network Theory employs a coercive critique of conventional and critical sociology. Nonrepresentational theory and transhuman constitute the basics of Actor-Network Theory. Science Fiction has emerged as one of the leading theoretical frameworks of ANT and Posthumanism in the 21st century. This is an attempt to envisage how ANT, Sci-Fi and posthumanism are interrelated and emerged step by step.

Keywords: Posthumanism, ANT, Sci-Fi Antihumanism, Cultural posthumanism, Philosophical posthumanism and post-human transformation.

Adjunction of Actor-Network Theory and Science Fiction in Posthumanism.

Posthumanism is a new way of apprehending the human subject in relation to the natural world in general. It is an anthropocentric and non-centred Cartesian dualism. Posthumanism champions a turning down of traditional Western humanism and here the bona fide study of man is the man. This places man at the centre of its literary and philosophical project. Most of the famous post humanists were largely engrossed with art, literature, historiography and philosophy.

Posthumanism is a rethinking of humanism. It makes over the concepts of classical humanistic ideologies and concepts. This is an enigmatic one, its 'post' prefix hints at the arrival of a new epoch. It deviates from the conditions of humanism. Actor-Network Theory is a theoretical and methodological approach to social theory where everything in the natural world exists in constantly shifting networks of relationships. ANT is a humanistic and anthropocentric perspective. It divulges the relevance of humans and technology in the post humanistic era. Posthumanism and ANT are hybrid networks, a heterogeneous conglomeration of humans and non-humans. It accentuates the materiality of humans and non-human and combines to produce purposes and particular effects.

All the strands are involved in a social state at the same level, and thus there are no external social forces beyond what and now network participants interact with at present. Social forces about exist in themselves and therefore cannot be used to explain social phenomena. Non-humans sort out to act or participate in systems or networks or both. And it is a forceful appraisal of regular and critical sociology. Actor-Network Theory began at the end of the 1970s. ANT is best understood from something that is performed rather than summarized. It is a complex concept. Everything is both an actor and a network. An actor whose activity is networking heterogeneous elements and a network is able to redefine and transfer what it is made of. Latour, John Law and others developed ANT, which chronicles social phenomena in terms of the interplay of human and non-human actors (actants).

ANT adds up to the rejection of borderlines that seemed to be secure in traditional humanist science and philosophy and has thus been an influential contribution to the posthumanist project ANT theorists want others to abandon dualism of action and intensions. But it is not so easy. Poststructuralism and deconstruction have the ideas of posthumanism. Their critiques use this concept. Critical posthumanism fuses openness to the radical nature of techno-cultural change and it highlights certain continuity with traditions of thought that have been critically engaged with humanism, which later evolved out of the humanist tradition in posthumanism. Posthumanism as a concept is similar to modernity that is cringing by definition.

Posthumanism and Science Fiction (Sci-Fi) rest on a utopian ideology that lies in being human, and utopia is always defined in relation to another. 21st-century everyday life popular culture is one constantly confronted with a post-human vision of technology 'next generation'. 'Sci-Fi' is often the relation of the transhuman which refers to the condition that is plausibly an extension and escalation of traditional humanism rather than its rejection. Science and technology studies and posthumanism arose as a loose disciplinary condition of sociologists, anthropologists, historians, and literary scholars. One of the important aspects of Sci-Fi is a technology and its whole humanity.

Technology is invented to make our lives easier though people feel nervous about technology. Interrogating humanity is an important theme in Sci-Fi where the concept of the posthuman view configures the human being.

Artificial intelligence is also a feature in many science fiction stories. Artificial life is used to raise questions about our real life. In posthumanism, the boundary is seen between the given and the constructed. Donna Haraway's *Cyborg Manifesto* (1985), declares that by the 'mythic time' of the late twentieth century we are all chimaeras, theorized and fabricated hybrids of machines and organisms. Bruno Latour and many other critics of STS have explained contemporary science for inconsistencies between its positivist rhetoric and its complicated and ambiguous practices. Latour argued for the breakdown of what he called the "modern constitution". This epistemology postulated many effective dichotomies, such as between society and nature and between human and non-human. To make the fearless genuine human race, the development of human advanced tools and efforts are necessary.

WORKS CITED

Herbrechter, Stefan."*Posthumanism A Criticasl Analysis*". Bloomsbury, 2018.

Ryan, Michael."*Actor-Network Theory*".sagepub.com-Ritzer-Entries14-July-2004.

Roger,Luckhurst,"*ScienceFictionStudies*".vol.33,No.1, TechnocultureandScience-FictionMar.2006.

BIO-NOTE

Sali S., Assistant Professor, Post Graduate Department of English, Don Bosco Colleg, Kottiyam, Kerala. She is an ardent lover of literature and her main areas of interest are

ELT, Gender Studies, Feminism and Trauma Studies. She has published two papers on gender identity and feminism.

CHAPTER VI

REPRESENTATION OF GENDER IN WOMEN'S MAGAZINES COVERS; A STUDY BASED ON VANITHA MAGAZINE

ABSTRACT

We examine the Cover pages of *Vanitha,* one of the most circulated women's magazines in India magazine, from January 2019 to August 2021 to find out the representation of women on cover pages. Content analysis is chosen as the method of research. Sixty-six cover pages from the *Vanitha* magazine were collected and analysed using descriptive statistics such as frequencies and percentages. The study also uses a visual analysis to examine the cover pages. The study's findings ascertain a stereotypical representation of women on the magazine covers. The study's findings implied that females got featured in women's magazines more. It is also found that even though the majority of the cover pages feature women, there is still a clear disparity in age, colour, class, and social status of the models featured. Women in their old age don't have any space on the cover pages.

In contrast, the middle and young women featured in the cover pages have been portrayed following the norms imposed by the patriarchal society. An accurate representation of the multidimensionality of the female psyche is absent on the cover pages.The study also finds out the current trend of women's magazines using single portraits as cover photographs. There is a recurring tendency to normalise the social norms established by the patriarchal groups regarding the ideal woman is evident in portraits of single women on cover pages. Most of the stars featured on magazine covers are actors, both Male and Female. It is followed by a significantly less number of models, politicians, singers and authors. It is also found that a seductive effect is visible in the pictures featured on the cover pages rather than communicating the content. The most dominant frame in cover lines is the health frame, followed by celebrities, beauty, food, relationship, career, festival, astrology, entrepreneurship, travel, and politics.

Keywords: Gender Representation, Content Analysis, Women Magazines, Kerala.

Introduction

Media have the power to reinforce, legitimate and naturalise norms in society. Media, especially mass media, play a significant role in projecting, propagating and normalising a constructed view of reality. The construction of reality in media is directly related to social power, cultural dominance and money. Media always tend to reinforce or establish the norms created by the above-mentioned influential groups' interests. Also, media is a vital agent in the cultural transformation of society. Through the media representations, the audience perceives themselves and the world(Fong, 2019).All media forms can control their consumers' emotions, thoughts, and social actions. But the degree of media influence will be varied according to the form of the media. The same content transferred to a particular audience group through different media platforms may impact them differently. An internet-based streaming application can create instantaneous reactions. Still, the in-depth approach and vivid detailing of the same content in a magazine has a different impact on its consumers. A well-researched and organised magazine's content has more credibility, and thus it has more influential power on its consumers.

Magazines play a vital part in socialising the cultural representation of society. In particular, Women's magazines can be seen as an essential avenue for gender identity and gender roles in developing nations like India(Das & Das, 2009). It is evident that the Indian periodicals have always raised women's issues in history. For example, Rajaram Mohanray's *Sambath kaumadhi* was the voice of the Anti Sathi movement(Pawar, 2008). In Kerala, women's magazines have also played a crucial role in educating women and questioning gender distinctions. The first women's magazine in Kerala was *Keraleeya Sugunabodhini*, published in 1887 from Thiruvananthapuram. And the first women's magazine edited by a woman was *Sarada*. *Mahila Ratnam, Lakshmibhai, Mahila, Mangalodhayam, Mahilamanthiram* are some of the early Malayalam women magazines published in Kerala. Women magazines in those days focus on spreading progressive ideas like education, employment, the necessity of ascertaining girls' desire concerning marriage etc.

Even though magazines were accessible to only a minority of the elite class and educated women during that period, more constructive discussions have emerged about women's empowerment through those magazines(SwarnaKumari, 2001). But today, regardless of the class, women magazines have access and acceptance among the readers in Kerala. The increasing number of women magazines and their circulation confirm the recognition. Some of the prominent Malayalam women magazines include *Vanitha, Grihalakshmi, Mahilaratnam,*

Kanyaka, Snehitha, Sthree dhanam, Mahila chandrika and much more. Women magazines have an imperative role in informing, educating, socialising and creating awareness among women. Kerala is a state with a solid matrilineal heritage, and it is also among the highest female literate state in India(Das & Das, 2009). Feminist academicians perceive a crucial role of women magazines in the upliftment and empowerment of Malayali women. So the impact and influence of women magazines on their readers are irrefutable. So it is indispensable to study the framing of gender and representation of women as it is concerned with the cultural metamorphosis of society.

Review of literature

Gender studies researchers have had a keen interest in the magazines and representation of women. Sammye & William G (1988) examines the cover pages of *Time magazine* from 1923-1987 to understand the representation of women in it. They perceive that women are underrepresented in the Time magazine covers during their study period. They have classified the women cover page personalities using age, nationality and occupation. Akinro & Mbunyuza-memani (2019) examined the depiction of African women in African magazines. Their findings implied that African magazines portray beauty identical to the western and white-centric beauty standards. Another similar study was done by Arakaki & Cassidy(2014), which observes the construction of fame and celebrity of the People magazine during the first decade of the 21st century. The results suggested that the people's magazine covers were mostly entertainers, accomplished or those who have dramatic personal lives. Fong(2019) did another study that betides in the Asian context he studies masculinity and feminity in Malaysian women magazines.

Their findings signify that Malaysian women's magazines encourage female readers to pursue their passion for promoting masculine and feminine characters essential for success. In the Indian context, Banerjee & Kakade (2018) examines the manufacturing of the concept of 'beauty' in Femina magazine. Their findings affirm the so-called patriarchal notion of women obsessed with fashion and beauty. In the Kerala context, Vinayan & Raj (2019) analyse the politics of 'ideal Malayalee women' in contemporary women's magazines. The study identifies the influence of patriarchy, caste and caste in the text of these publications. The study also ascertains the underlying politics in their apolitical stance. Even though there are studies related to the framing of women in magazines, the extent of gravity of the issue makes it relevant to discuss. Furthermore, most of the studies focusing on Western magazines, which are entirely different from the Indian and especially Kerala.

To bridge this gap, we propose a study with the following objectives.

Research objectives

To classify the cover pages of *vanitha* women magazines based on gender.

To find out the type of cover photographs in women magazines

To identify the people on Cover pages in terms of their profession

To determine the frames of cover stories in women magazines

Research questions

RQ1 Who got featured on the *Vanitha* magazine cover pages in terms of gender?

RQ2 What type of celebrity got featured on the *Vanitha* magazine cover pages?

RQ3 What are the trends in cover photographs in terms of the type of cover?

RQ4 What frames were employed by the cover stories in women's magazines?

Research Method

Content analysis is chosen as the method of research. The magazine selected was *Vanitha* which was launched in 1975. *Vanitha* is a fortnightly Malayalam women magazine that is a part of the Malayala Manorama group. The magazine had a readership of over 2 million, making it one of the highest-read magazines in India. The researchers analyse all covers of *vanitha* magazine published from January 2019 to August 2021. Sixty-six cover pages from the *vanitha* magazine were collected and analysed using descriptive statistics such as frequencies and percentages. The researchers also use visual analysis to interpret the cover pages. The researchers use the Magazine Covers as the unit of analysis to answer the first three research questions. Walter (2019) identifies the importance of magazine covers and cover lines. He acknowledges magazine covers as an 'independent, self-contained unit'. The cover can both be editorial and social indicators of importance.

The researchers categorise the gender of cover page models, type of cover page photographs and type of people on the cover page in terms of the profession to determine the research objectives. Coding for the gender of cover page models, cover photographs by type, and type of celebrity in cover photographs on cover pages was done through a detailed visual inspection of the cover pages. Coding categories chosen for gender were 1, Male only,

2, Female only and Both. Coding categories for the cover photographs by type were 1, Single, 2, Couple and 3, Group. Celebrity type was also coded in the same fashion with Five categories 1, Actors; Persons best known for their acting in films and serials. 2, Musicians; Individuals who are known for their talents in singing and music. 3, Models; Individuals best known for their work posing for photographers and artists. 4, Politicians; Individuals who are famous for their activities in government and political parties. 5, Authors; Individuals known for their writing skills. Along with the coding, the researchers critically evaluate the cover pages to identify their underlying trends.

The researcher uses the cover lines as the unit of analysis to answer the last research question. "What frames are employed by the cover page stories in women magazines?" This study uses an inductive approach for analysing frames. The coding categories are designed after a preliminary examination of the samples. As a result of the initial examination, 12 frames were identified.

1, Health; Focuses on physical and mental health

2, Celebrity; Discussing the famous personalities

3, Beauty; Emphasizing makeup and beauty tips

4, Politics; Discussing government, political party leaders

5, Education/Career; Emphasizing Jobs, Courses, and learning-related

6, Travel; Discussing travel experiences and unique travel spots

7, Food; Focussing on food /cooking and kitchen

8, Festival; Focussing on the festivals like Onam, Christmas and Ramzan etc

9, Astrology; Horoscope and stars signs related

10, Relationship; Focussing on Marriage, Love and family

11, Entrepreneurship; Businesses and Market related

12, Success stories; Achievement stories of women

Two of the authors worked as the coders for this project. If there arouse questions and discrepancies in coding, the authors discuss them. The authors use additional materials like books, magazines, newspapers and the Internet to resolve the issues. An intercoder reliability test was conducted even if all the issues were resolved through discussions. The author code all the 66 covers, and the results were not disclosed before being compared. Using Holsti's formula for intercoder reliability, the level of agreement for gender was 1.0, the level of agreement for the type of cover photo was 1.0, the level of agreement for the celebrity type was 0.98, and the level of agreement for the frames was 0.96.

Among the 66 cover pages of Vanitha magazine published between January 2019 to August 2021, 66% of the cover pages are women, while 6% are men, and 27% include both men and women (refer to table 1). The results are not surprising as the magazine *vanitha* is meant for women. So it is quite natural that more women appear on the cover pages. There are no transpersons' among the 66 cover pages analysed. As we strive for a gender-neutral society, and media have a massive role in altering our culture, our media should change to give a fair representation of transpersons on their contents.

Another important observation is that even though most cover pages feature women, the samples' stereotypical representation is evident. All the women featured on the cover pages have similarities in age, colour, class, and social status. We found that all the women featured on the cover pages of *vanitha* magazine are very young. A majority of them are in their twenties and look healthy and energetic. Women of age in between their thirties and forties are also got a commendable representation. The women in this category are often represented as homemakers - a social position, the patriarchal society forcefully imposed over the women community. The women in their old age are not featured in any of the cover pages of *vanitha*. Thus, we can argue that the so-called women-oriented magazines are only interested in creating a pleasant and energetic feel. Not all age groups are placed on the cover pages, which means an accurate representation is absent in the content also.

An apparent disparity is evident in the models' skin tones portrayed on the cover pages. All the models, especially the women featured on the cover pages, are white-skinned, which shows that the women magazines are trying to reinforce or normalise the idea of the patriarchal world. *Vanitha* is a magazine circulated in Kerala, where most of the population is brown or dark-skinned. Even then, they try to establish white skin as a symbol of beauty and pride. These stigmatic representations expose the superficiality and dishonesty of the so-called women magazines in Kerala.

The researchers identified a severe paradox in the class, and social status of the women featured on the cover pages. All the models featured represent an affluent class. The costumes, ornaments, and total setting of the picture approve the above argument. The researchers concluded from these assumptions that even though most of the cover pages feature women, there is still an apparent disparity in the featured models' age, colour, class, and social status. This kind of representation will help the dominant male society reinforce their viewpoints on the women's community.

Conclusion

This study tries to answer four intriguing research questions related to women magazines. Which gender got featured in women magazine covers? What types of photos are included in cover photos of women magazines? What kinds of personalities are featured on the cover pages of women's magazines based on the profession? What are the frames used in cover lines of women magazines?. The study's findings implied that females got featured in women magazines more. Yet there are instances of Male only covers and covers featuring both Male and Females. It is also found that even though the majority of the cover pages feature women, there is still a clear disparity in age, colour, class, and social status of the models featured. Women in their old age don't have any space in the cover pages. In contrast, the middle and young women featured in the cover pages have been portrayed following the norms imposed by the patriarchal society. An accurate representation of the multidimensionality of the female psyche is absent in the cover pages observed.The study also finds out the current trend of women magazines using single portraits as cover photographs. It is followed by group and couple photos which are comparatively fewer.

There is a recurring tendency to normalise the social norms established by the patriarchal groups regarding the ideal woman is evident in portraits of single women on cover pages. The paid promotion of the textile and jewellery can also be viewed in the single portrait representations. We have an interesting finding regarding the type of celebrities featured in women's magazines. Most of the stars featured on magazine covers are actors, both

Male and Female. It is followed by a significantly less number of models, politicians, singers and authors. It is also found that a seductive effect is visible in the pictures featured on the cover pages rather than communicating the content. Our study finds out the frames of the cover lines of the women's magazines. The most dominant frame is the health frame, followed by celebrities, beauty, food, relationship, career, festival, astrology, entrepreneurship, travel, and politics. Apart from some of these compelling findings, our study has some limitations too. We do not measure the effect of this framing on the readers. We hope future researchers will try to find out the impact of magazine framing on the audience. Despite these drawbacks, we hope our research will contribute significantly to the study of framing in women's magazines. Also, it will help to bridge some gaps in gender studies in magazine research.

Works Cited

Akinro, N., & Mbunyuza-memani, L. (2019). Black is not beautiful: Persistent messages and the globalization of " white " beauty in African women's magazines. *Journal of International and Intercultural Communication, 12*, 308–324. https://doi.org/10.1080/17513057.2019.1580380

Arakaki, J., & Cassidy, W. P. (2014). "Defining Celebrity and Driving Conversation": Celebrities on the Cover of People Magazine (2000–2010). *Journal of Magazine Media, 15*(1). https://doi.org/10.1353/jmm.2014.0017

Audit Bureau of Circulation. (2019). *Highest Circulated amongst ABC Member Publications (across languages) As certified up to 22nd February 2019.* Retrieved from http://www.auditbureau.org/files/JJ2018 Highest Circulated amongst ABC Member Publications (across languages).pdf

Banerjee, S., & Kakade, O. (2018). Construction of the ‘ Beauty ’ concept: An Analytical Study of Femina – A Leading Women ’ s Magazine. *JMSD*, (March 2018), 69–76.

Das, H., & Das, M. (2009). Gender Stereotyping in Contemporary Indian Magazine Fiction Gender Stereotyping in Contemporary Indian Magazine Fiction. *Asian Studies Review*, *33*, 63–81. https://doi.org/10.1080/10357820802713593

Fong, Y. L. (2019). Gender representation and framing of Malaysian women: A study of feature articles in the female magazine. *Journal of Content, Community and Communication*, *10*(5), 29–38. https://doi.org/10.31620/JCCC.12.19/04

Pawar, N. (2008). Women ’ s Magazine Tanishka: A Study. *Karnatak University Journal of Humanities*, *47*, 50–62.

Sammye, J., & William G, C. (1988). Women Through Time: Who Gets Covered? *JOURNALISM QUARTERLY*.

SwarnaKumari, E. K. (2001). WOMEN'S ’ MAGAZINES IN KERALA AND THEIR SOCIAL SIGNIFICANCE. *Indian History Congress*, *62*, 705–708.

Vinayan, S., & Raj, M. S. (2019). The politics of representation and the “ ideal Malayalee woman ”: Remembering Malayalam women’s magazines of the early 20th century. *Journal of Postcolonial Writing*, *55*(3), 399–411. https://doi.org/10.1080/17449855.2019.1570966

Walter, A. (2019). On the cover of the rollin’ stone how rolling stone magazine frames politics and news. *Journal of Magazine Media*, *19*(2), 25–49. https://doi.org/10.1353/jmm.2019.0013

CHAPTER VII

BAPSI SIDHWA'S THE PAKISTANI BRIDE: A FEMINIST STUDY

Devika Singh
Ph. D. Research Scholar
Central University of Haryana.

ABSTRACT

The Pakistani Bride, written by Bapsi Sidhwa, a well-known Pakistani novelist, is a notable work in the field of feminism. Sidhwa's goal in the work is to show the silent parts of domestic abuse in the marriage, in which women play a minor role. The protagonist, having firsthand knowledge of the challenges that women confront in a patriarchal society, refutes the sacrosanct notion of marriage, in which women are ensnared by various social regulations created by male representatives of society. This study makes an attempt to present all of the social conventions and techniques that males use to subjugate women through the ostensibly sacred institution of marriage. Sidhwa emphasised that the marital system is designed to suit the needs of men, whether they are physical or sexual. Marriage is not pre-planned in heaven, but it is in a patriarchal society that restricts women's independence.

Bapsi Sidhwa's *The Pakistani Bride*: A Feminist Study

Mary Wollstonecraft initially addressed the feminist themes of gender disparity and inequality in her book *A Vindication of the Rights of Women* (1792). Virginia Woolf explored and posed comparable themes in her novel *A*

Room Of One's Own (1929). With the publication of Simone de Beauvoir's *The Second Sex*, the feminist wave grew even stronger (1949). In her book *Sexual Politics* (1970), Kate Millet emphasised the biological nature of sex and the social construct of gender. Toril Moi's *Sexual/Textual Politics* (1985) and Sandra Gilbert and Susan Gubar's *The Madwoman in the Attic: The Woman Write*r and the Nineteenth-Century Literary Imagination made significant contributions in this regard (1979).

Feminism developed into a specialised and systematic field of study. The lines between phallocentric and gynocriticism were drawn. Phallocentric principles predicated on 'woman' are presented in literature from the perspective of male authors. The feminist era is thought to have ended in the 1970s, while the post-feminist era began in the 1980s. Since ancient times, women's connection to nature has been undeniable. Ecofeminism arose from the bond between women and the environment. *Surfacing* by Margaret Atwood is an example of this style of specialism. For feminine works, the French used the term "ecriture feminism."

Gynocriticism is "a French term that refers to criticism primarily obsessed with the inspiration, creation, and analysis of writing by women on women," according to N.Krishnaswami. In the paper, 'Feminist Criticism in the Wilderness' Showalter manifests that, "the first task of gynocritic criticism must be to plot the precise cultural locus of female literary identity and to describe the forces that intersect an individual woman writer's cultural field." Thus a gynocritical reading of *The Pakistani Bride* would be 'palimpsest'(1) in nature. Patrocinio P. Schweickart says, "today, the dominant mode of feminist criticism is 'gynocritics', the study of woman as a writer, of the 'history, styles, themes, genres, and structures of writing by women; the psychodynamics of female creativity...".

Women are prisoners and victims in Islamic society's sex-role paradigms, according to a gynocritical reading of *The Pakistani Bride*. Feelings of weakness and subjection in women set the path for insurrection. An isolated hill village inhabited by Pakistani Islamic tribes' is the setting at the beginning and end of the tale. Here, tribal laws and punishments are in effect. Cut off from modern culture, the style of life, conduct, and thought has become archaic. The patriarchal or phallogocentric culture.

The novel begins with a delicate depiction of women's subordination and epitomises the man (even as a toddler) as the master of sexual and physical strength. Resham Khan, unable to repay the loan, gives Qasim's father his daughter, Afshan. Afshan is considered a commodity rather than a person. Qasim's father considers marrying Afshan because he only has one wife, but due to a "twinge of paternal conscience," he marries Afshan to Qasim, who is only ten years old. She finds out she was married to a boy on her wedding day and asks, ``Are you, my husband?" She questioned incredulously, and Afshan couldn't decide whether to laugh or cry. She accepts her fate, and her relationship with Qasim is more like that of a mother than that of a spouse. Marriages are decided by the menfolk in this country, and women have no voice in the matter. As if everything were predestined, they simply accept and harmonise with the situation.

Female marginalisation is a common occurrence in Pakistani society, as men seek to keep their women hidden from men's gaze. Qasim dismisses Nikka, ``don't ask a hill-man anything about his womenfolk, understand? I would slit your throat ...."(Sidhwa,36). Strangely all vulgar and disgraceful terms are connected to one's mother and sister,``... incestuous lover of your mother, lover of your sister, son of a whore ..."(Sidhwa,42).

In the ambience of the city of Lahore watching Zaitoon Miriam says," she'll (Zaitoon) be safe only at her mother-in-law's ....a girl is never too young to marry"(Sidhwa,53). Thus, the moment a girl reaches adolescence, marriage in the eyes of the society, is the *summum bonum* of a woman's life as Semone de Beauvoir writes in *The Second Sex*, ``marriage is the destiny traditionally offered to women by society"(Beauvoir,445). A woman is supposed to be the man's possession. The development of a woman's personality is discouraged. She is reminded that she is unique in comparison to men. After her menstruation, Miriam instructs Zaitoon after her menstruation, "you are now a woman. Don't play with boys and don't allow any man to touch you. This is why I wear a burkha..."(Sidhwa, 55).

A woman is not even permitted to enter a mosque to offer prayers under Islamic practice, ``the men .... Gathered in mosques ... the women ... prayed silently for the duration of the call carrying on with whatever they were doing, stirring the pot in the kitchen or breast feeding the baby"(Sidhwa, 58).

Qasim observes a horrific scene while visiting a brothel. A pimp forced a prostitute to perform contortions in order to perform dancing routines. Unfortunately, the fatigued and exhausted woman was unable to express her sexuality, ``the woman continued her monotonous, mechanical spasms, one hip jerking higher, jaws dribbling spittle ....A man obscenely shaking his body called to her as to a monkey (Sidhwa, 65).In reality, this advice is intended to extort money from her rather than to protect her honour.

Chapter 10 opens up with the statement, ``marriages were the high points in the life of the women``(Sidhwa, 88). The zenana, or special quarters for women, are found in Islamic residences and allow them to move freely without veils or burka. Qasim delivers his promise to Misri Khan, a companion from his native land, at a wedding. He arranges her wedding without even asking Zaitoon's opinion. Miriam was sensitive to realise it, she quips, ``how can a girl, brought up in Lahore, educated – how can she be happy in the mountains? Tribal ways are different, you don't know how changed you are ....They are savages. Brutish, uncouth, and ignorant! She will be miserable among them"(Sidhwa, 93).

Despite constant warnings from Miriam about Zaitoon's unhappy future Qasim goes ahead with his decision. Even Zaitoon complies without putting up a question . Zaitoon respected her father's decision and, "a blind excitement surged through her "(Sidhwa, 96). On Miriam's advice, ``tell your father you don't want to marry a tribal. We'll help you" (Sidhwa, 98). Zaitoon expresses her inability to cross her father.

Carol, the American wife of Farukh wrote to her friend Pam, "I love Lahore.... I don't feel programmed! The people are kind and hospitable. I'm having a ball" (Sidhwa, 108). But this was a veneer. Farukh often accused Carol of, "displaying your honky-tonk pedigree! You laugh too loudly. You touch men ....Don't you know if you only look a man in the eye it means he can have you?" Farukh's enmity bordered on insanity. He was always curious about her daily routine while he wasn't around. Farukh's replies reveal a woman's fragility in the absence of a male presence to shield or defend her. In his absence, he suspected other men of taking advantage of Carol's westernised lifestyle. A

"... male is fortunate in having opportunities for releasing his impulse to domination and the fury of his frustrated ego because he always has a wife whom he can treat as an inferior" (Mill, John Stuart, 40).

Another officer, Mushtaq, was drawn to Carol. The three tribesmen burst out laughing and making wicked catcalls as they saw them in a compromising situation. Carol is embarrassed by the male attention.``The obscene stare stripped her of her identity. She was a female monkey, a gender opposed to that of the man – charmless, faceless, and exploitable" (Sidhwa, 120).

Carol is upset by Farukh's brash behaviour. Carol is impressed by Zaitoon's hesitancy while probing him about marriage at the officer's mess. Farukh's unkind remark, ``our women, particularly the young girls, are modest, you know "(Sidhwa, 133). This remark not only offends her, but it also alienates her; the phrase "our women" clearly excludes non-Pakistanis, including Carol in this case. As Qasim reveals Zaitoon's separation from her true parents during the division days, Zaitoon begins to cry. Carol forms a female bond with Zaitoon and expresses her sisterly compassion for her by offering her a shawl and food.

Mushtaq, who was acquainted with tribal culture, knew that a woman was a symbol of status, the symbol of a man's honour, and the focal point of his job as a provider for tribals. A woman is only viewed in the context of a male. As Gilbert and Gubar observe in The Madwoman in the Attic, she has no independent existence. To be selfless is not only admirable but also to be dead.

Zaitoon notices the tribal people's 'savagery and harshness' instinctively. Her background and education in Lahore make her revolt and she tells Qasim, ``that jawan at the camp, Abba, I think he likes me. I will die rather than live here"(Sidhwa, 157). Zaitoon becomes selfless' as a result of Qasim's harsh scolding. She is willing to marry Sakhi and live with him. After marriage a girl cannot maintain her individuality, ``there is a unanimous agreement that getting a husband – or in some cases, a 'protector' is for her the most important of undertakings....She will free herself, from the parental home, from her mother's hold; she will open up her future not by active conquest but by delivering herself up, passive and docile into the hands of a new master"(Beauvoir, 352). Zaitoon's tantrums and reclusive behaviour are unwelcome in the family. Yunus Khan warns Sakhi, ``she requires a man to control her"(Sidhwa, 170). Wife battering is accepted, Sakhi not only beats Zaitoon,``you are my woman! I'll teach you to obey me!"(Sidhwa, 172-173) but also Hamida, his mother. Following this occurrence, Zaitoon became sure that she would not live long.

The existence of a woman is determined by the service she can provide to a man. Marriage is the beginning of a pitiful period of women's marginalisation. A woman is portrayed as a tool for a man to have sexual delights..``Slowly Carol had begun to realise that even among her friends, where the wives did not wear burqas or live in special, women's quarters, the general separation of sexes bred an atmosphere of sensuality. The people seemed to absorb it from the air they breathed "(Sidhwa, 112). Though Carol came from a highly liberated background, she also understood that ``men here expected subtlety from women "(Sidhwa, 112).

During Carol's affair with Mushtaq, she never realises that ``he was having a fling, merely killing time"(Sidhwa,179). But later she realised that his attraction towards her was due to, his ``long separation from his family, his need for a woman in the loneliness of his remote posting"(Sidhwa, 180). Mushtaq's attitude does not change even after Carol slaps him. For Mushtaq, Carol was only a sex object. He no longer found her sexually provocative .``... in every age, a woman has been seen primarily as mother, wife, mistress and as a sex object in their roles in relationship to man"(Ferguson 4-5).

In the hills, Zaitoon did not have the freedom of moving around unwatched. Sakhi furiously beat her up abusing her as, ``you dirty, black little bitch, waving at those pigs ..."(Sidhwa, 185 ). Zaitoon had to beg for mercy and on that particular night, Zaitoon resolves of running away as,`` she knew that in-flight lay her only hope of survival. She waited two days, giving herself a chance to heal"(Sidhwa, 186). There is a limit to how much pressure and sublimation can be applied to something. Zaitoon's life takes a U-turn at this point, as she bravely flees to a place that is hostile to her. Rather than showing care for the bereft lonely woman, society fuels the fire. In culture, a woman is revered only if she has a husband at her side, yet the runaway zaitoon antagonises her spouse and is raped in another town while she is alone. She has cornered like a 'flustered hen' and a man whispers to her, ``you can't escape us, my dove" (Sidhwa, 214). Even at this point, Zaitoon does not give up she continues her chase in search of her promised land. After her own rape at Lahore, "abandoned and helpless, she had been living on that charity of her rapists ... and on theft"(Sidhwa, 231).

Meanwhile, Carol in her room with Farukh feels, that "women the world over, through the ages, asked to be murdered, raped, exploited, enslaved, to get impregnated, beaten-up, bullied and disinherited. It was an immutable law of nature. What had the tribal girl done to deserve such grotesque retribution?"(Sidhwa, 226)Carol recalled her Pakistani female acquaintances who appeared to be westernised but appeared melancholy, probably due to Islamic countries' rigid narrow-mindedness regarding women. Zaitoon was miraculously saved, and the tribal men are overjoyed at the news of her death. ``Misri Khan's massive shoulders straightened. He thrust his chest forward and his head rose high. It was as if a breeze had cleared the poisonous air suffocating them and had wafted an intolerable burden from their shoulders."(Sidhwa, 244).

Sidhwa eloquently demonstrates that a guy in society is not only physically strong but also a skilled manipulator in the power game through the storey of Zaitoon. Despite the fact that a woman is neither physically stronger nor adept at manipulating the power game, Zaitoon's khudi (will strength) may be a sign of societal transformation.

I would like to quote a verse by Iqbal on Khudi

Khudi ko kar buland itna - Heighten your khudi touch majesty

Ke har takdeer say pahaylay- That before every turn of fate

Khuda banday say poochay - God himself asks man

Buta teri raza kya hai? - Tell me what you wish?

WORKS CITED

Sidhwa, Bapsi. *The Pakistani Bride.* New Delhi: Penguin, 1990

Beauvoir, Simone de. *The Second Sex.*Harmondsworth: Penguin,1983.

Mill, John Stuart "The Subjection of Women".*Women's Liberation and Literature,* ed. Elaine Showalter. Harcourt Brace, 1971.

Fergusson, MaryAnn. *Images of Women in Literature.* Houghton Mifflin : Co-Boston, 1973.

CHAPTER VIII

THE OTHER SIDE OF MULTICULTURALISM: VIOLENCE IN GLORIA NAYLOR'S THE WOMEN OF BREWSTER PLACE

Ms. Aashlesha. V. Lele

ABSTRACT

Multiculturalism can be defined based on its dual reception on the social front. The ideal utopian expectation remains a far-fetched dream in reality. The African American writer Gloria Naylor highlights this negative discourse of multiculturalism and sets her novel 'The Women of Brewster Place' in the typical multicultural background, presenting a diverse socio-cultural society. Along with highlighting the plight of the Women implicitly, the paper also thrives on bringing out the lopsided view of multiculturalism, issues of the multicultural society, the existential struggle and troubled experiences of 'the coloured folks', particularly black women. The paper essentially delves into the territory that presents the other side of multiculturalism, especially in the African American context, with predominant issues related to identity, sexuality, racism and psychological degeneration.

Keywords: Multiculturalism, Social Violence, Racism, Discourses of Multiculturalism

INTRODUCTION

Multiculturalism as a concept is predominantly concerned with the diversity of perspectives. Like every moment and idea, multiculturalism too has various aspects and facets. Some advocating the positive stance view multiculturalism as a compatible seamless intermingling of different cultures while others consider it a utopian delusion - a potential threat to a coherent national identity and secularism, thereby fostering discrimination based on race, culture, ethnicity and colour. The present paper rejects the former ideas to solely focus on the negative aspects of multiculturalism in a particular socio-cultural community and in the desired coherent multicultural nation in general. Countries like Canada witnessed the success of multiculturalism, whereas the visible adverse effects of the same were experienced in Germany and United Kingdom. The impact of multiculturalism, both direct and indirect, can be seen in writers from various parts of the world, especially those living in multicultural societies. Focussing more on the undesirable aspects, this paper plans to study multiculturalism in an unfavourable setting, presenting it as a significant barrier to the coherent national identity, thereby leading to its fragmentation. This discussion will focus on how multiculturalism leads to violence, trauma and destruction.

The United States of America, a multicultural nation, is often referred to and interpreted as a "Salad Bowl", which has had a very traumatic past. Its traumatic history of slavery, racism and implementation of racial discrimination has hindered the nation's 'true assimilation'. In The Women of Brewster Place (1982), the African American novelist Gloria Naylor, focusing on the dominant feminist themes of the life and experiences of black women also deals with the issues of violence that seem to pose its roots on adversities of multiculturalism. Various episodes in the novel highlight the issue of violence which is seen manifesting itself through the complexities of multiculturalism, viewing its adverse effects that led to psychological distortions, identity crisis and physical abuse among the people of a particular ethnic group. Through this fictional setting of Brewster place, the author is capable of successfully dealing with the real-life issues, retelling how the stings of racism and wounds of segregation has divided the human race, leading to destruction and degeneration." Prejudice" according to Maya Angelou 'is a burden that confuses the past, threatens the future and renders the present inaccessible.' It won't be wrong to say that every writer from a multicultural background of 'the coloured' race expresses this burden of the past accompanied by confusion, chaos and unrest in his / her works. Speaking to Angels Carabi in one of the interviews, Gloria Naylor talked of her personal experience of racism and segregation which was felt in a direct manner in the South while in the North it was disguised in the air of subtlety, as she says "Racism here was more subtle" (1991, p. 24). In another interview with Ashford, speaking on the racial segregation of her nation the author says "I think we're still struggling under the scars of slavery, and I think that the Civil Rights Movement did not work. The country is almost as divided as before" (2005, p. 74-75).

The trauma of psychological abuse

The novel witnesses one of intense psychological damage caused in the character of Kiswana Browne, a mixed race offspring born of a white father and a black mother, a condition that pulled her still closer to experience a continuous clash of culture, both within and around her. Though she is an outcome of the union of black and white parents, she is always drawn towards the black. She celebrates and asserts her negritude and her being a black. She knew that Black is something to do with negativity, yet she overlooks the fact and takes pride in everything that would contribute to her identity as a black. Regarding such obsessions with one's own identity, Amartya Sen in his book Identity and Violence: The Illusion of Destiny proclaims, "A sense of identity can be a source not merely of pride and joy, but also of strength and confidence" (Sen, 2007, p.1). The way in which Naylor presents the character of Kiswana is very interesting. Kiswana is of a light complexion with straight hair. Dissatisfied with her physical attributes, she often seen complaining to her mother for her physical dissimilarity with her race that does not project her as a black. She actively participates in all sorts of revolutions for the emergence of black republicans in college. In order to resemble a 'negro' and achieve a sort of assimilation with her roots, she tries to curl her hair and even changes her original name Melanie to adopt a name that sounds more African– 'Kiswana'. Kiswana's conversations with her black mother, bring out her psychological rage and the emotional turmoil when she says:

"Oh, God, I can't take this anymore. Trying to be something I'm not–trying to be something I'm not mama! Trying to be proud of my heritage and the fact that I was of African descent. If that's being what I'm not, then I say fine. But I'd rather be dead than be like you–a white man's nigger who's ashamed of being black!" (TWBP, 1983, p. 85)

Amartya Sen, also while discussing the negative aspects of such identical obsessions writes, "And yet identity can also kill and kill with abandon. A strong–and exclusive–sense belonging to one group can in many cases carry with it the perception of distance and divergence from other groups" (Sen, 2007, p.1-2). This proves to be true in the case of Kiswana. Her obsessions about her identity and her strong sense of belonging with the 'blacks' strengthen her rage and incompatibility towards the whites or any other racial or cultural groups. On the contrary, her physique prevents her from identifying herself with the blacks, eventually her psyche refrains her from relating herself to the whites as well. It manifested itself into a state of "identity disregard" according to which an individual is seen continuously "ignoring" or "neglecting"any sense of identity with others (Sen, 2007, p. 20).

Gloria Naylor, through her male characters like Fuller and Woods tries to portray the ever-persisting intense psychological turbulences of what she calls it, to be a "scarred psychology" (Ashford, 2005, p. 86). These characters of colour in Naylor's The Women of Brewster Place, seems to be deeply affected by the prevailing adverse notions of Colonialism and Euro-Centrism. The notions which, since ages have developed a negative impact on the minds of a black, colonizing their psychology and accordingly streamlining their thoughts. Thus the thought of a man of colour regarding himself and his physical appearance is always shaped on negative grounds, generating a kind of shame for himself and his entire race. This is the result of the deep-rooted psychological upheaval taking place among the blacks as a result of racism.

Apart from the "scarred psychology" of Kiswana, this implicit form of long-condensed and genetically-transmitted psychological abuse is seen in the daily conversations and dialogues of these male characters like Butch Fuller and also in the prayers of Reverend Woods. For instance, in a conversation between Mattie Michael and Butch Fuller (in the 1st section of the novel entitled 'Mattie Michael'), while they were walking under the scorching sun of April and Fuller was trying to protect his skin from getting dark in the sun, he asserts, "Too much sun on the main road,[...] And since black means poor in these parts–Lord knows, I couldn't stand to get no poorer" (p. 12). A similar outcome of the deep seated psychological violence is cited in the speech of Reverend Woods when he, while in the process of preaching delivers these lines, "Yes, Lord–grind out the unheated tenements! Merciful Jesus– shove aside the low-paying boss man. Perfect Father fill me, fill me till there's no room, no room for nothing else, not even that great big world out there that exacts such a strange penalty for my being born black" (p. 65).

This way, Naylor extends the Euro-centric notions of blackness through the dialogues and thoughts of her characters that are so much burdened with the load of such notions in the form of psychological violence that they are bound to reflect through their daily conversations and psychologies. Here violence resulting from racism in the form of psychological destruction is seen as a driving force for the generation of dialogues in the novel.

The "unstringed puppet": sexual violation and racism

In the novel, the problem of multiculturalism is subtly dealt with a biangular discourse in section entitled "The Two". While the first angle is grounded in the context of the differences in skin colour of 'the two', the second is fueled by the uncanny sexuality shared between 'the two' women. Here, "The Two", stands both as a suitable title for a particular section in the novel as well as for the lesbian couple– Lorraine and Theresa. Naylor is very particular in her description of the external features of these two characters. She describes Lorraine as "the lighter, skinny one" who was "readily accepted" (p. 129) by the women of Brewster Place. Theresa on the other hand, is described as "the short dark one--too pretty, and too much behind",for whom "breaths were held a little longer" (p. 129). The phrases apparently tend to be describing the physical attributes of the two ladies. Though at a deeper level, it is a more racist approach abusing the doctrine of multiculturalism. The bodies of these women, therefore become a reflection of one's own (racist) perception, the stereotypes governing human existence, as it is truly said that, "women's bodies [the black women in particular], in patriarchal societies, are fashioned into conventional notions of femininity, and if the body resists the disciplining process, "subtle coercion" is exercised" (Ghosh et al., 2017, p. 219).

Lorrain's "lighter" skin color and "skinny" body type associate her more to a white occidental woman than to a black woman of color. On the other hand,

Theresa's "dark" complexion and "short" body type with "too much behind" associates her with a woman of color, thereby projecting her as the typical oriental women of the East. A more realist approach of the portrayal reflected racism when the author describes Theresa pertaining to the stereotypical norms of a black female body objectifying and presenting it as something that the black feminist critics like Hooks term it to be "transgressive", "promiscuous" or "sexually deviant" (Hooks, 1982;

Young, 2007), when Naylor further writes, "And she insisted on wearing those thin Qiana dresses that the summer breeze moulded against the maddening rhythm of the twenty pounds of rounded flesh that swung steadily down the street" (p. 129-130).

Apart from their opposing physical appearance both Lorraine and Theresa participate equally in the bond of homosexuality that exists between the two. Lorraine, because of her skin color and body type that resembles the occidental woman is viewed as an 'other's-other' in the conservative black society of Brewster Place. In relation to the multicultural context, Lorraine is viewed under two lights, one as an 'occidental' and the other as a 'lesbian', where both sets her culturally out of the mainstream. Even though Theresa's black body is stereotypically viewed as something that Hooks calls "expendable" with its "accessibility" and "availability" (Young, 2007, p. 13) the trauma of rape befalls solely upon the shoulders of Lorraine, assuming her to be the most suitable victim. By violating Lorrain's "tall" and "yellow" body, C.C. Baker and his friends consider that they have culturally overpowered the "others". This ironical ideology of cultural overpowering is reflected through the dialogues of Baker when he persistently abuses Lorraine while raping her, "I am gonna show you somethin' I bet you never seen before." C.C. Baker takes the back of her head, presses it into the crotch of his jeans, and jerkily rubs it back and forth while his friends laugh, "Yeah, now don't that feel good? See, that's what you need. But after we get through you, you aren't never gonna wanna kiss no more pussy" (TWBP, 1983, p. 170).

Such abusive lingual addressing reflects a faulty cultural overpowering of patriarchy over heterosexuality (lesbianism) where the former tries to restore his lost hegemony over the latter through sexual violence. This idea of violence against gay and lesbians is dealt with in one of the sections (entitled 'Violence against Gay and Lesbian People') in Beckett and Macey's essay Race, Gender and Sexuality: The Oppression of Multiculturalism". According to this analysis, the society and its people (in particular those adhering to the Qu'ran and the Bible) "see it as their duty to physically harm people who are not heterosexual" (2001, p. 313). While regarding the physical (ie., the racial and color) context, the rape of Lorraine reminds us of the episode of the rape of Lynne in Alice Walker's Meridian. Like the rape of Lynne,

Lorrain's rape too, can be read as a black man's fallacious act for his "need to liberate himself from white oppression by taking revenge upon white women" (Lauretqtd. in Tanritanir and Aydemir, 2012). The other female characters in the novel, like Ben's daughter Etta, and Mattie too, endure sexual violations in the garb of either slavery or marriage or may be through the expression of momentary love. While Ben's daughter embraces sexual harassment by a white master as a compromise at the hands of her poverty, Etta is used for physical gratification by Woods suggesting false intentions of marriage. Also, Mattie is made to offer her virginity to Butch just to fetch his thirst that always lusted for her "full round breasts" (p. 17) and "high round behind" (p. 9).

In all the cases of rape and sexual assault of these women of Brewster Place the root cause of violence is seen to be arrested in issue of multiculturalism that attacks the harmonious cultural hybridity of a society nurturing racism and intolerance. While Lorraine's rape was a result of racial intolerance, the sexual use of Ben's daughter, Etta and Mattie depicts the racial segregation of black women projecting them as what Hooks calls the most "undesirable" yet the most "accessible" beings as per the established Euro-centric norms (Hooks, 1982). Black men tend to rape their own women in their own frustrations as a result of their "scarred psychologies" that generates from these cultural differences. While dealing with the atrocities inflicted on the black women, the writer intends to "touch(es) upon the larger black feminine sensibilities. She narrates the lives of these women with a purpose– to legitimize their female self, its history and culture. In the process of unraveling the hidden histories of the characters, she invents a new poetics" (Sonal and Singh, 2017, p. 209).

CONCLUSIONS

According to critics like Markus, Plaut, Wolsko et al., the notion of multiculturalism was established to stress on the importance of cultural diversities, the recognition of diverse ethnic, racial and cultural groups and the explicit valuing of this diversity in the mainstream settings. This traditional ideology, though many a times seemed to fail in achieving its proposed goals. According to Plaut's unfavorable concept of multiculturalism, it is defined as something that stands in contrast to the so assumed concept of 'color-blindness' that overlooks any existing differentiation in terms of one's skin colour. Multiculturalism thus celebrates differences, intolerance and violence. A report on multiculturalism under the study of American Nationalist Party, read by the heading, 'Multiculturalism, Racism, Violence and Balkanization', attacks its ideology of racial differences claiming multiculturalism to have been at its strongest when racism is at its best. It also proclaims that multiculturalism is the highest form of racism. Writers have taken this issue as a nexus for their discussion to portray one's historical, social and personal predicaments. In the case of some of the black female writers and black women in general, it goes "indisputable that their own victimization has led these women towards social activism" (Das and Singh, 2016, p. 219). Though, multiculturalism projects its diverse discourses both good and bad, Gloria Naylor still finds herself and her entire race struggling under the scars of racism and slavery (Carabi, 1991). Her novel The Women of Brewster Place thus projects the problem of multiculturalism that degrades the larger human race necessarily leading to violence, thereby portraying violence as en embedded discourse of Multiculturalism.

REFERENCES:

1. Ashford, Tomeiko R. (2005). "Gloria Naylor on Black Spirituality: An Interview".

MELUS, 30(4),7387.Retrieved from http://www.jstor.org/stable/30029635

1. Beckett, Clare. and MarieMacey (2001)."Race, Gender and Sexuality: The Oppression of Multiculturalism". Women's Studies International Forum 24(3/4), 309319.

3. Carabi, Angels. (1991). "Interview with Gloria Naylor."Revista de Estudios Norte americanos.n., 23-35.

4. Das, Ankita. and Rajni Singh (2016)."Empowering Lives: The Journey of Jaycee Dugard, Elizabeth Smart, and Mukhtar Mai" .Journal of Dharma 41(1), 201-220.
5. Ghosh, Soumya M. and Rajni Singh.(2017). "Violated Bodies and the Reclamation of Female UshaGanguli's Ham Mukhtārā and Maya Krishna Rao's Walk".Archiv Orientalni 85,219-252.
6. Hooks, Bell (1982). Ain't I A Woman: Black Woman and Feminism. Pluto Press:

London. Print.

7. Naylor, Gloria. (1983). The women of Brewster Place. U.S.A: Penguin books.

Subjectivity in

8. Niru Sharan, Violence Against Women and the Laws in India, IMPACT:

International Journal of Research in Humanities, Arts and Literature (IMPACT: IJRHAL), Volume 5, Issue 7, July 2017, pp. 197-202

9. Sen, Amartya. (2007). Identity and Violence: The Illusion of Destiny. U.S.A: Penguin Books.Print.
10. Sonal, Smrity.and Rajni Singh (2017)."Black Female Bodies and Resistance in

Gayl Jones' Corregidora and Eva's Man".Rupkatha: Journal on Interdisciplinary Studies in Humanities9(2),203-211.Retrieved from https://dx.doi.org/10.21659/rupkatha.v9n2.21

11. Tanritanir, Bulent C.and Y. Aydemir (2012). "The Suffers of Black Women in

Alice Walker's Color Purple and Meridian and Toni Morrison's Novels Beloved and The Novels the Bluest Eye".The Journal of International Social Research 5(23).437-444.

12. Rajesh Kumar MD, Domestic Violence Against Women in Indian Context:

Causes and Impact on Family, IMPACT: International Journal of Research in Applied, Natural and Social Sciences (IMPACT: IJRANSS), Volume 5, Issue 8, August 2017, pp. 27-34

13. Young, Tiffany Ann (2007). Rape in Contemporary American Literature: Writing

Women As Florida State University)Electronic Theses, Treaties and Dissertations. Paper 868.

14. Sonal, Smrity and Singh, Rajni, Violence, an Embedded Discourse of Multiculturalism in Gloria

Naylor's *The Women of Brewster Place* (February 3, 2018). IMPACT: International Journal of Research in Humanities, Arts and Literature, Vol. 6, Issue 2, February 2018, 257-262 , Available at SSRN:https://ssrn.com/abstract=3133494

CHAPTER IX

A STUDY ON MYTH AND NARRATION IN NAGA-MANDALA

***Ann Hermina Christy, **Suryanarayana Menon & ***Sachin S.**

University Institute of Technology, Pathiyoor Regional Centre

Department of English, University of Kerala.

INTRODUCTION

Naga - Mandala is a beautiful play written by the great author Girish Karnad. *Naga - Mandala* is inspired by two folk tales told by A. K. Ramanujan, the eminent indologist, the playwright has composed this piece of writing dealing extensively with metamorphosis. Metamorphosis means a complete change of a character. In *Naga-Mandala,* it is the Naga- a snake, who changes his appearance into Appanna (the protagonist's husband), to be with Rani (the protagonist). The Naga, Appanna, and Rani are all characters of the story. An allusion to one of the main characters who is a Naga, a popular deity mainly in rural India, portrayed in mythology as half-human, half-snake. *Naga – Mandala* is the name given to a ritual snake dance performed in the coasts of Karnataka, a south Indian state which Girish Karnad belongs to.

Girish Karnad is an Indian film actor, a director and a Kannada writer. He was born *in* Chitra Pura Saraswat Brahmin family of Matheran, in present day Maharashtra. Karnad initial schooling was in Marathi. Later his father was transferred to Sirsi in the Kannada speaking regions of Bombay presidency. Karnad was exposed to travelling theatre groups. Travelling theatre groups is an independent theatre that is presented at a different location in each city. He was also a Jnanpith awardee who predominantly worked in south Indian cinema in Bollywood. His rise as a playwright and marked the coming of the modern age of Indian play writing in Kannada.

A Study on Myth and Narration in *Naga-Mandala*

The play *Naga-Mandala* is derived from folk-lore. In this play, Karnad turns away from the 'classical' traditions to the local Kannada folktales as his source. It is based upon two orals Kannada tales he had heard from his mentor friend and well-known poet and translator, A. K. Ramanujan, to whom, he also dedicated the play. Here, Karnad combines two tales - the flame story, and the story of Rani and Appanna. Karnad's *Naga-Mandala* is based on two oral tales from Karnataka, as we know from what he says in his 'Introduction' to three plays, "these tales are narrated by women – normally the older women in the family while children are being fed in the evenings in the kitchen or being put to bed The other adults present on these occasions are also women" (4).

The word 'Naga-Mandala' is derived from a Sanskrit word 'Nagama', which means beautiful and charming woman. The story includes many mythical creatures who are the ones who says the story. In *Naga-Mandala*, Girish Karnad uses elements from traditional theater to weave together two oral tales handed down by woman storytellers. The mythical creatures are the narrators of the story. It is from the mythical creatures' stories that new stories arise. Myth refers to colourful stories that tell about the origin of humans and the cosmos. As stories, myths articulate how characters enact an ordered sequence of events. According to the common misconception of the term myths are merely primitive fictions, illusions or opinions based upon false reasoning. It is also believed that myths have developed out of folktales. According to M. H. Abrams:

Folktales have been normally understood as traditional verbal materials and social ritual that have been handed down primarily by r, word of mouth. Folktales developed and continued to flourish best in communities where few people can read or write. It includes, among other things, legends, superstitions, songs, tales, proverbs, riddles, spells, nursery rhymes; pseudo-scientific core about the weather, plants and animal. (63)

In reality, mythology includes much more than grade school stories about the Greek and Roman deities or clever fables concocted for children's enjoyment. As Mark Schorer in *William Blake: The Politics of Vision*, says "Myth is fundamental, the dramatic representation of ourdeepest instinctual life of a primary awareness of man in the universe, capable of many configurations, upon which all particular opinions and attitudes depend" (6). According to Alan W. Watts, "Myth is to be defined as a complex of stories (some no doubt fact and some fantasy) which for various reasons human beings regard as demonstrations of the inner meaning of the universe and of human life" (9). The ironical part is that the character called 'the story' is the one who says the main story. The story is about Rani a beautiful young girl who is married to Appana a rich young spoiled man. Throughout the entire story we get a glance of different theories. There are a few dialogues in the story that has more than one theory that can be applied to it. We see almost three stories in the play.

Karnad has named the characters just according to their roles. He named the main character, Rani, which means 'queen'. From the incidents in the story, Rani is almost like a queen itself. He named the next character, Rani's husband as Appanna, which means 'any man'. The contrast in the names also shows the contrast in the characters roles in the play. Rani is finally treated even better than a queen and to such an extent that she is almost treated like a Goddess. As said earlier all narrated by mythical creatures. The characters in the play are: the man, the flames, the story, rani (queen), Appanna (any man), Kurudavva (The Blind One), Kappanna (The dark one) and Naga (which means the cobra).

The play *Naga- Mandala* can be analysed from different points. If we start from the prologue itself, we see aspects of myth used. Myth is defined as a traditional story, especially one concerning the early history of people or explaining a natural or social phenomenon and typically involving supernatural beings or events. *Naga -Mandala* unlike other plays also has a prologue. In the prologue we see a man sitting in the temple and trying his level best to fight death. We get to know that from the following lines.

Man: I may be dead within the next few hours. I am not talking of 'acting dead'. Actually dead. I might die right in front of your eyes. A mendicant told me: 'you must keep awake at least one whole night this month. Every night this month I have been dozing off before even being aware of it. I am convinced I am seeing something with these eyes of mine, only to wake up and find I was dreaming. Tonight, is my last chance. This huge monologue is the first myth that leads us to other myths in the story. This monologue can be classified as a classical myth as it has all the characteristics that a myth requires. The monologue is extremely important because it is from this one large monologue that we move onto the other myths in the story. (2)

While this man sits there, he sees a few flames walking in and speaking in the voices of women. Seeing this instance, he says "I don't believe it! They are naked lamp flames! No wicks, "No lamps" (2). As said earlier such an instance qualifies as a myth. Then again, we get to see the flames having a conversation, where a lot of new flames are introduced. The flames are made as flame1, flame 2, flame 3, flame 4 and so on. The flames then discuss their own problems. The flames come every night after all their work is done. We can understand that from the following dialogue by flame1: The master of our house, you know what a skinflint he is! He is convinced his wife has a hole in her palm, so he buys all the groceries himself. This evening, before the dark was even an hour old, they ran out of kusbi oil. The tin of peanut oil didn't go far. The bowl of castor oil was empty anyway. So, they had to retire to bed early and I was permitted to come here. Such an event is not seen in reality and this can also be qualified as a myth. (2)

Later on, a new flame arrives and says:

You know I have only an old couple in my house. Tonight, the old woman finished eating, swept and cleaned the floor, put away the pots and pans, and went to the room in which her husband was sleeping. And what should she see, but a young woman dressed in a rich, new sari step out of the room! The moment the young woman saw my mistress, she ran out of the house and disappeared into the night. The old woman woke her husband up and questioned him. But he said he knew nothing. Which started the rumpuses. (3)

This is the dialogue that led to the next myth which we are about to go through. To the earlier dialogue another flame asks, "who the young woman was and how did she get into the house?" (4). Now then the new flame replies:

My mistress, the old woman, knows a story and a song. But all these years she has kept the story them to herself, never told the story, nor sung the song.so the story and the song were being choked, imprisoned inside her. This afternoon the old woman took her usual nap after lunch and started snoring. The moment her mouth opened, the story and the song jumped out and hid in the attic. At night when the old man had gone to sleep, the story took the form of a young woman and the song became a sari. The young woman wrapped herself in the saree and stepped out just as the old lady was coming in. Thus, the story and song created a feud in the family and were revenged on the old woman. (4)

This dialogue in the play gives us an exact representation of what a myth is. These incidents we see her are something that we can never see in reality. It is from this myth that the character called 'the story' who is an important figure in the play. It is from this character 'story' that Rani's story arises from here that we get the concept of, 'a story within a story'.

Once again in the play we get to see another myth in act in. In the scene where Rani meets Kurudavva, she tells Rani about how she got her husband and in that story that she tells Rani comes the next myth. As kurudavva says:

I was born blind. No one would marry me. My father wore himself out going from village to village looking for a husband. But to no avail. One day a mendicant came to our house. No one was home. I was alone. I looked after him in every way. Cooked hot food specially for him and served him to his hearts content. He was pleased with me and gave me three pieces of a root. And said any man who eats one of these will marry you. (12)

This story that Kurudavva says also qualifies as a myth as it has the characteristic of the traditional aspect of a myth. This is also the story that leads to the unimaginable events that take place in Rani's life. We get to see by now that all the myths are interconnected. One of the biggest or rather the main part of the story involves the shape changing, here we can we Naga changing into Appanna at night. It is an age-old belief that cobras can take any form. We understand it from the lines said by the story, "As you know a cobra can assume any form it likes. That night it entered the house through the bathroom drain and took the shape of" (18). From these lines we can again qualify this incident as a myth as it involves the supernatural aspect of the myth.

As we know a social phenomenon involving a supernatural event also qualifies as a myth. Towards the end we see Rani getting questioned for being pregnant as Appana her real husband claims he has never touched her, which is actually true. As we know it is Naga that has touched Rani, but she as well as Appanna is not aware of this. So, because of this Appanna makes it a huge problem in the village to such an extent that Rani has to prove her innocence through ways that are unimaginable. This is where we come across one of the biggest myths in the play.

We get to know about this from the following lines when Naga tells Rani, "Then listen to me carefully. when you face the elders, tell them you will prove your innocence. say you will undertake the snake ordeal" (34). To which Rani replies, "what ordeal?" (34). Here is where the biggest or rather one of the most important or rather one of the most significant myths of the play lies. As Rani is expected to hold the cobra that lies in the ant hill, in order to prove her purity. Rani is frightened initially, but is advised by Naga to hold the cobra and speak only the truth. Rani very easily escapes this ordeal as she says, "since coming to this village, I have held by hand, only two'. And then proceeds to say, 'my husband and this cobra. Except for these two I have not touched any one of the male sexes. Nor have I allowed any other male to touch me. If I lie, let the cobra bite me" (39). These incidents that Rani had to undergo can be classified as a typical myth.

In act two, we get to see the relationship between Rani and the Naga. The starting dialogue itself shows how Naga gets close to Rani: Rani is sleeping and Naga is watching her from a distance, exactly as at the end of Act One. "He moves near her and then gently caresses her. She wakes up with a start. Rani- You-you; Naga: don't get up, Rani: But when did you come? shall I serve the food. And so on" (8). From this we can also categories this as a myth as such an incident is not something that happens in real life.

Apart from myth we can also take a note of its narration. Narration is defined as the action or process of narrating a story. Narration can be taken from different points of view: from first person, from second person, and from third person. By first person point of view, it typically means that the protagonist says the story. By second person or from second persons point of view the author uses a narrator to speak to the reader. And by third person point of view, it's the external narrator who tells the story. Here the first-person narrative includes the narrator himself.

Here in this play, there are different points of view of narration as said earlier. All the perspective of narratives are interconnected. This play includes a story within a story model, so as the story progresses, we get to see or rather hear stories from different characters that enter. The main point that we can point out is that all the stories are interconnected. From the very first, in the prologue, the character referred to as, 'The man' is the narrator'. He is the same person who introduces the other characters as well. We can understand that from the following lines, "I don't believe it! They are naked lamp flames! No wicks, no lamps. No one holding them. Just lamp flames on their own- floating in the air! Is that even possible? (2). From these lines we find that he is not only talking about himself but also introducing the other characters in the play. Another notable element in the play are the four different narrative levels. Narrative levels are an analytic notion whose purpose is to describe the plurality of narrating instances within a narrative. On the first narrative level, the flame story is about the playwright who has to stay awake for the whole night in the temple, to let the cure pass.

The second narrative level includes mythical elements. The author- narrator meets the host of the giggling flames, each one carrying her own story becomes the second story. These personified flames go to the same ruined temple where the author-narrator is bewailing his plight. The third narrative level is a tale by a flame, who wants to be forgiven for arriving late to the hosting place. The tale is about an old woman who knew an interesting story but refused to share it with others. Ironically that story slipped out of the snoring old hags' mouth and is transformed into a beautiful young lady and the song that accompanies it, turns into a beautiful sari. The fourth narrative level is the story of Rani, the lady who was born out of the story from the old hag's mouth. Rani becomes the main character of the play. As the main story begins the complex turn in the structure of the story can be observed.

Another aspect that can be observed in the story is the aspect of betrayal. We can find many levels of betrayal here. A) the husband betraying the wife- we get to see how Appanna Ranis husband even though had Rani, went out to his concubine. Appanna was a spoiled rich man who thought he could do anything he likes. Not only did he betray her by meeting his concubine but also betrayed her by locking her up in the house and not allowing her to speak to anyone. B) Wife betraying the husband- although this is something that Rani does unknowingly to her husband, it is marked as a betrayal to which she gets pregnant. The second betrayal here is that she hides the fact from her husband the child is not his in order to live a calm life with him. Appanna is forced to look after the child. C) The next betrayal that we see here is the supernatural being, that is the snake, betraying the couple- the snake fools Rani by taking the shape of her husband and fools the husband by giving Rani a child and also helping her to escape the consequences of his mistake. D)The son betraying the mother- here Kurudavva loses her son to someone who comes and takes her away: this is her explanation as to what happened to him;

If only I had my eyes! I would have seen her. I would have recognized. but what can one do with these pebbles? when he tried to tell me I didn't listen. I was deaf. A temptress from beyond? A yaksha woman- perhaps a snake woman? But not a human being. No. what woman would come inside our house at that hour? And how? She wasn't even breathing. I shouted: 'who are you? what do you want from us? Go away!' suddenly the door burst open. The rushing wind shook the rafters. He slipped from my hands and was gone. Never came back. (38)

From these lines we get to know that he left her and ran away. The play is so diverse that we get to analyse and understand and even predict different aspects of the same play. Another aspect that we can analyse in the play is the shape shifting aspect of it. In the beginning we get to see the flames taking on human shapes to gossip at the temple after they have been put out in their houses. Another shapeshifting scene is when the new flame says:

You know I have an old couple in my house. Tonight, the old woman finished eating, sweeping and cleaned the floor, put away the pots and pans, and went to the room in which her husband was sleeping. And what should she see, but a young woman dressed in a rich, new saree step out of the room! The moment the young woman saw my mistress she ran out of the house and disappeared into the night. The old woman woke her husband up and questioned him. But he said he knew nothing. Which started the rumpus. (3)

Shape-shifting, metamorphosis, and transformation are important mechanisms in folk-tales and literature throughout the world. Use of these terms, specifically the term shape-shifting generally means a person or creature who is able to change their shape at will or by the aid of another. Shape-shifters may be evil or benign depending on the need created in the story for their particular talents. Shape-shifters may change their shape by some inner magic ability, through a magic object, or by ingesting something which causes the transformation. To which the flames replied, "But who was the young woman? How did she get into your house?" (4).

The general purpose of shape-shifting in folk-lore and literature is to blur the distinctions and portray the collapsing boundaries between the human and the animal world. "It is offered as both punishment and reward, mortality and immortality, ugliness 1 and beauty. Tales of shape-shifting project our human anxieties regarding identity, worth, isolation, and the very notion of what it means to be human" (2). It is also and sometimes most importantly used to depict a mental and spiritual change in a person. Overall shapeshifting is linked to power. Those in control of their shape exercise power over the natural world those who are unwillingly transformed are subject and enslaved. Transformation into an animal is usually a tragic fate. It is neither death nor life, but a state of limbo. It degrades the human to a nonhuman status, brought about by a witch, a god, or the sorcerer's apprentice. These are the lines that show us the shapeshifting aspect of the play.

The shapeshifting aspect plays an important part in the story. The next shapeshifting aspect in the play that is about to be discussed is actually the most important one as it created the most drama in the play. The shapeshifting of the Naga into Appanna, we understand that from the following lines: story: As you know, a cobra can assume any form it likes. That night, it entered the house through the bathroom drain and took the shape of the cobra takes the shape of Appanna.

To distinguish this Appanna from the real one, we shall call him Naga, meaning a cobra. This change is what puts Rani in a dilemma as to what she is experiencing is true and it is the same thing that makes Appanna think that Rani is cheating on him. Another shape shifting aspect that we get to see in the story is Rani who is apotheosized into a living goddess after the cobra ordeal. We get to see that from the following lines, "Appanna, your wife is not an ordinary woman. She is a goddess incarnate. Don't grieve that you judged her wrongly and treated her badly. That is how goddesses reveal themselves to the world. You were the chosen instrument for revealing her divinity" (40). It is through these lines that we get to see Rani's transformation.

Another great aspect that we get to see in play is 'Divinity', here Rani is portrayed as a divine character when she is put to the test to see whether she is lying or not. Rani, my husband and; Appanna: And say, who else? Rani: And this cobra, yes, my husband and this king cobra. Except for these two I have not touched anyone of the male sex. Nor have I allowed any other male to touch me. If I lie let the cobra bite me" (39). The cobra slides up her shoulder and spreads its hood like an umbrella over her head. "The crowd gasps. The cobra sways its hood gently for a while, then becomes docile and moves over her shoulder like a garland. Music fills the skies. The light changes into a soft, luminous glow" (39). Rani stares uncomprehending as the cobra slips into the ant-hill. There are hosannas and cheers from the crowd. "Elder1: a miracle! elder 3: indeed, a goddess" (39). It is from this scene in the play that we get to divine nature or divine aspect of Rani. Although this is classified as a myth it can also be classified as 'divinity'.

In act one there is a particular scene that depicts the 'social caging' that Rani undergoes. As it quotes 'Rani jumps up with fright. Hurriedly mixes the paste into the milk. comes out and gives Appanna the glass of milk. He drinks it in a single gulp. "Hands the glass back to her. Goes to the door, ready to put the lock on. She watches him intently. This shows how rani is stuck in her own house and not allowed to go anywhere" (40). This also depicts how some people are considered lower than others and are put in imaginary cages. Here Rani is in an actual cage not allowed to go out or even talk to anyone. Another even that can be categorised as social caging is an event that includes

Rani being questioned and asked to go through horrible punishments to check if she is pure or not.

Another aspect that we can see here is the infidelity of man and woman. Before we go into the actual part or the main interpretation, let us look at another interpretation that is possible. While Rani is put to the test to know if her baby is actually Appanas, kurudavva comes running saying that her son is missing and the exact words she says is that, "I woke up. It was midnight. I heard him panting. He was standing up Stiff like a wooden pillar. Suddenly I knew. There was someone else in the house. A third person" (38). From these lines we can also interpret that Kappanna, kurudavvas son was actually Rani's lover. As the time he goes missing and the time Rani is caught is the same. This is just an interpretation as most of the story lines point to Naga itself as her lover. But this interpretation is much more realistic when compared the story of Naga.

Another infidelity here is that Appanna is openly unfaithful to Rani when he goes daily to his concubine, leaving Rani alone at home. The same way rani is unfaithful to Appanna but is unaware of it because the Naga takes the form of Appanna when he comes to meet her. But in the end when Rani tries to give the Naga his proper rights as a father it is actually an unfaithful act to Appanna because he is forced to look after his son that is actually not his. We understand that from the following dialogues by Rani:

When we cremate this snake, the fire should be lit by our son. To which Appanna says: as you say. To which rani then says: and every year on this day, our son should perform rituals to commemorate his death. This is one act of unfaithfulness by Rani. There is one more incident that shows this. That incident is in the second ending. When Rani and Appanna finds a cobra in Rani's hair, the dialogue

Rani says shows the second infidelity: Rani: (softly to the cobra) you? What are you doing here? He'll kill you. Go. Go away. No! Not that way. He's there. What shall we do? What shall we do? Why did you come in here stupid? My hair! Of course. Come, quick. climb into it. Quick now. Get it. Are you safely in there? Good. Now stay there. And still lie there. You don't know how heavy you are. Let me get used to you, will you? (44).

These lines show how Rani tried to save Naga, but once again indirectly cheats Appanna. In both the endings Rani is quite unfaithful to Appanna. Another aspect that we can analyses in the story is the dual ending. In the first ending Naga enters Rani's bedroom again and dies for the sake of her and her family's happiness. we see that in the following lines; Naga:

Rani! My queen! The fragrance of my nights! The blossom of my dreams! In another mans arms? In another mans bed? Does she curl around him as passionately every night now? And dig her nails into his back? Bite his lips? and here I am- a sloughed off skin on the top of a thorn. An empty sac of snake skin. No. I can't bear this. someone must die someone has to die. why shouldn't I kill her? if I bury my teeth into her breast now, she will be mine- mine forever. (Moves swiftly towards her but stops). 'No, I can't. My love has stitched up my lips. Pulled out my fangs. Torn out my sac of poison. Withdraw your veils of light, flames. Let my shame float away in darkness. Don't mock gecko. Yes, this king cobra is now no better than a grass snake. Yes, that is it. A grass snakes. A common reptile. (42)

From the above long monologue by Naga is the idea of the first ending. Naga decides to kill himself because he cannot bear the thought of losing his loved one. His extreme sadness and his thoughts of suicide and also the scene of him killing himself is portrayed in these lines. Then later on we get to know that Naga is dead from the next set of lines said by Appanna when Rani asks him to comb her hair and this is how he replied; "Appanna: 'certainly. (He combs her hair. He has to struggle to get the comb through. A dead cobra falls to the ground) a cobra stays away" (43). This is how the play ends for the first time. But the flames were sad and dissatisfied with the unhappy ending and so now the 'man' tries to give an alternate ending.

Here once again Rani cries that her head is hurting, but this time Appanna finds a live snake instead of a dead one. When Appanna tries to kill it, Rani asks the sake to get into her hair and hide there. Then Rani, her husband, her child and the snake live happily ever after. We get to see this ending from the following lines;

Appanna: a snake! Stay away! Its tiny but it's a cobra, all right. And alive. How did it get into your hair? Thank God for your thick tresses. They saved you. Wait. We must kill it; Rani: softly to the cobra: you? What are you doing here? He'll kill you. Go. Go away. No! not that way. He's there. What shall we do? What shall we do? Why did you ever come in here? Stupid? My hair! Of course. Come, quick. climb into it. Quick now. Get it. Are you safely in there? Good. Now stay there. And lie still. You don't know how heavy you are. Let me get used to you, will you? (45)

And that is how the second ending came. It is not like usual stories with a single ending but a story with a dual ending which makes it much more interesting than other stories. The entire play can be analysed from different aspects. Even the same dialogue has more than one aspect that can be analyzed from it. The majority of the play relies on the aspect of myth. But that is not the only aspect we get from the play. We also get aspects of a) narrative technique b) shape-shifting c) infidelity among husband-and-wife d) divinity e) betrayal-five stages of betrayal and f) dual ending.

As said earlier all these aspects are taken from the same dialogues sometimes. The play is so diverse that each time we read it we read it, we get the feeling of reading it again and again. Each time we ready the play we get different concepts from the same lines we read once before. The concepts included in the play show what a great writer karnad was, as he not only included one concept but many for the readers to analyse and understand. The concept of infidelity is actually an eye opener as we get a hint of reality from the concept itself.

But as we know most of the other concepts are solely based on myth so the concept of reality basically has no place. And also, that particular interpretation basically disrupts the whole myth concept itself. So, it is safe to say that the concept dominating the play is actually myth. But the other interesting parts like shapeshifting and divinity all indirectly contribute to the concept of myths. We may get a different interpretation but it all leads us back to the idea of myth. Indirectly myth and narrative techniques are the main concepts.

Works Cited

Primary source:

Girish karnad, Naga- Mandala, oxford university press

Secondary source:

Abrams. M. H. Glossary of Literary Terms. 7th Ed. Macmillan, 1995.

Mythological Aspects in Girish Karnad, *Naga-Mandala Karnad*, Girish. Author's

Introduction Plays: Naga-Mandala, Haya Vandana, Tughlaq. 1994.

Karnad, Girish. Naga-Mandala: A Play with a Cobra. 1990

CHAPTER X

TRAUMA AND ITS MANIFESTATIONS IN THE KITE RUNNER

***Asha Krishnan, **Siyana Sulaiman, ***Ashid, & ****Anshad**

University Institute of Technology, Pathiyoor Regional Centre

Department of English, University of Kerala.

INTRODUCTION

Khaled Hosseini has become a prominent writer for his realistic representation of his homeland, Afghanistan. His stories are set against the background of Afghanistan's history, culture, tradition, and ethnic diversity. Though his novels narrate the traumatic life journey of the Afghans, the theme in his novels is not confined to that country, rather it highlights the hardships, struggles, and journeys that are common between various nations and cultures. He was born in 1965 in Kabul, Afghanistan. Hosseini graduated from Independence High School in San Jose in 1984 and enrolled at Santa Clara University, where he earned a bachelor's degree in biology. Then he worked as a physician in California. The success of *Kite Runner* helped him to retire from the medical profession in order to pursue writing. Hosseini is best known for his three novels *Kite Runner* (2003), *A Thousand Splendid Suns* (2007), *And the Mountains Echoed* (2013).

In all his novels Hosseini masterfully depicts the prevalent socio-political condition of Afghanistan. He exposes to the world the atrocities faced by the Afghan people and the mental states of its victims. *A Thousand Splendid Suns* are set in the war-torn neighbourhood of 1990's Kabul. It is an epic story of three generations of Afghan women and their remarkable resilience. The central characters are Laila and Mariam. The novel clearly shows the patriarchal despotism where women are dependent on men in all stages of their life.

Trauma and its Manifestations in *The Kite Runner*

The word "trauma" is derived from the Greek word "traumatizo" which means "wound". Trauma studies began in the 1860s, as clinicians began to notice victims of railway accidents having prolonged and unusual reactions that extended beyond their physical injuries. However, it was not until the 1880s that doctors began psychological examinations of primary women suffering from odd behaviour with no apparent cause. The works of early psychoanalysts did much to bring to light these women's mental conditions. In *Beyond the Pleasure Principle*, Freud describes trauma as a mental disturbance of survivors' devastating events which involve a risk to life, such as railway disasters, accidents, or the terrible war which has just ended.

According to the American Psychological Association (APA), trauma is "an emotional response to a terrible event like an accident, rape or natural disaster." However, a person may find any event physically or emotionally threatening or harmful. A traumatized person can feel a range of emotions both immediately after the event and in the long term. They may feel overwhelmed, helpless, shocked or have difficulty processing their experience.

When a child feels intensely threatened by an event he or she is involved in or witnessed, we call that event a trauma. There is a range of traumatic events to which children and adolescents may be exposed. They are bullying, community violence, early childhood trauma, physical abuse, refugee trauma, sexual abuse and traumatic grief etc. Initial reactions to trauma can include exhaustion, confusion, sadness, anxiety, agitation, numbness, dissociation, and physical arousal.

Although the concept of trauma is borrowed from psychoanalysis and psychotherapy, over the past century trauma has also become a key term in cultural criticism and literary theory. In *Unclaimed Experience: Trauma, Narrative, and History*, Cathy Caruth (1996), one of the most innovative scholars of trauma theory, defines trauma as "the response to an unexpected or overwhelming violent event or events that are not fully grasped as they occur, but return later in repeated flashbacks, nightmares, or other repetitive phenomena" (9). In her book, *Trauma Fiction*, Anne Whitehead (2004) for the first time applied trauma theory to literary texts and examines the literary representation of trauma and describes how trauma fiction, emerged along with trauma theory as a way to "elaborate on the ethical and cultural implications of trauma" (4) and explores the "politics, ethics and aesthetics" (3) of remembering. As studies of trauma became more common, the term has been applied more liberally to circumstances beyond those initially imagined-such as war, natural disaster, abuse and confinement to include psychological trauma that might not have resulted in physical violence.

The book *Trauma and Literature* (2018) by J. Roger Kurtz has attracted a great deal of interest in literary studies. As a key concept in psychoanalytic approaches to literary study, trauma theory represents a critical approach that enables new modes of reading and thinking. It is a leading concept of our time, applicable to individuals, cultures, and nations.

The representation of trauma in fiction often faces the danger of falling into the “fact versus fiction” trap. A trauma novel includes a definite realistic and historical dimension and is often based on documents and testimonies. The reader of this type of fiction may search for the exact representation of his/her traumatic experience, expecting to find the discussion of similar emotions and consequences. Thus, authors who take up the topic of collective trauma face many challenges: these novels examine the transpersonal dimension of collective memory that spreads beyond the individual and across an entire culture.

Trauma fiction is often based on the memories of experiencing a personal or collective traumatic event; thus, usually, the fictional narratives of collective trauma explore both personal and collective dimensions. A trauma narrative always includes the reader, whose role may be that of a person whom the victim/narrator confides or one with whom the victim/narrator shares the traumatic experience. Often a direct reference to the setting (time and place) serves as a unifying password in the recognition of trauma. The term "trauma novel" refers to a work of fiction that represents an emotional and/or cognitive response to profound loss, disaster, disruption, or devastation on the individual or at the collective level.

Here we discuss the representation of trauma in the narrative, *The Kite Runner*. Through a close reading of the novel, the aim of the present chapter is to analyse how trauma is narrated in the novel and thus try to have a better understanding of Afghan history and life. Though almost all characters in the novel go through a traumatic experience, it is beyond the scope of this chapter to analyse the traumatic journey of each and every character. So, the attempt would be to focus mainly on Amir's character to analyse how trauma works at the individual level. Moreover, the collective manifestation of trauma is also examined through analysis of the representation of the Hazara community. Hence, the present study focuses on the manifestation of trauma at the individual and collective levels.

Amir is the protagonist of this story. He is a sensitive and intelligent son of a businessman in Kabul. Throughout the novel, we can see different shades of character in Amir. Initially, he is presented as selfish, sensitive, and cowardly but later in the novel, he becomes brave and caring. Amir is also trying to change himself to atone for what he has done in the past. Hence, we see a shift in their personality of Amir from the

Individual trauma generally arises from some personal experience and attacks the victim with unexpected suddenness and consequences. In *The Kite Runner*, Khaled Hosseini complicates protagonist Amir's personal trauma by depicting him as a victim and a sinner. Amir is tormented by the guilt of abandoning his friend Hassan, who actually is Amir's half-brother. When Hassan is beaten and raped by Assef and the other two local bullies in an empty street, Amir did not do anything to help him. Although Amir is physically unharmed, the traumatic memory of his cowardice and betrayal haunted his later life. The traumatic effect of the rape has severely haunted Amir's normal life. He constantly suffers from the symptoms of post-traumatic stress disorder (PSTD): nightmares, avoidance symptoms, hypervigilance, disturbed sleep and distracted mind etc.

I thought about Hassan's dream, the one about us swimming in the lake. There is no monster he said, just water. Except he'd been wrong about that. There was a monster in the lake. It had grabbed Hassan by the ankles and dragged him to the murky bottom. I was that monster. That was the night I became an insomniac(93-94).

Amir's traumatic experience as a witness to the sexual assault on Hassan generates an indelible effect on his psyche. This in turn alters the normal relationship with Hasaan. Before the incident, Amir and Hassan are intimate friends like a carrot and pea.

When we were children, Hassan and I used to climb the poplar trees in the driveway of my father's house and annoy our neighbours by reflecting sunlight into their homes with a shard of mirrors. We would sit across from each other on a pair of high branches, our naked for dangling, our trouser pockets filled with dried mulberries and walnuts. We took turns with the mirror as we ate mulberries, pelted each other with them, giggling, laughing (3)

On the contrary, after that accident, Amir suffers from the impact of trauma brought by shame and guilt and undergoes violent mood swings. One day Amir asked Hassan to go up the hill and told him he wanted to read him a new story. They sat against the low cemetery wall under the shade thrown by the pomegranate tree. To Hassan's great surprise, Amir picked up an overripe pomegranate and hurled the pomegranate at him.

Amir also deliberately avoids the person and things associated with the sexual assault, which results in his hysteric behaviour of telling a lie to drive Hassan away from his home. On the day after his birthday party, Amir hides his new watch in Hassan's bed to frame the boy as a thief and force his father to fire Hassan's father Ali. But his behaviour does not release his conscience from recalling his traumatic experience, instead, his sense of guilt worsened.

I wanted to tell them all that I was the Snake in the grass, the monster in the lake. I wasn't worthy of his sacrifices: I was a liar, a cheat, and a thief. And I would have told, except that a part of me was glad. Glad that there would all be over with soon. Baba would dismiss them, there would be some pain, but life would move on. I wanted that, to move on, to forget, to start with a clean slate. I wanted to be able to breathe again (115).

Amir's shame and guilt follow him after he and his father escape to the United States, where he attends college, gets married, and becomes a successful novelist. The wound of trauma is not healed until Amir returns to Taliban-ruled Afghanistan and risks his own life to rescue Sohrab, Hassan's son from the evil Assef, a Taliban "monster". Thus, when Assef beats Amir, he feels: "My body was broken.... but I felt healed. Healed at last. I laughed" (303). Finally, by rescuing Sohrab, Amir reaches his personal redemption and healing.

While the story is told from Amir's point of view who is the witness to childhood sexual abuse, the narrative remains effective in portraying the victim's trauma as well. The author explains Hassan's post-traumatic stress disorder through changed sleeping patterns. Hassan started spending more time sleeping in the daylight as it temporarily helped him erase the memories of trauma. Hassan used to sleep to escape from the pain induced by trauma. Hassan embraced sleep as soon as he was done with his chores.

Sleep is often used as a coping mechanism for trauma. It is because during sleep the world and its problems cease to exist for conscious human minds. The challenges begin again when an individual wake up from sleep. Apart from the change in sleeping patterns, Hassan's post-traumatic stress disorder included reduced eating. Hassan had not been eating well and taking care of his health resulting in him becoming weak and losing weight. His physical weakness has been stated as "Hassan looked tired too - he'd lost weight and grey circles had formed under his puffed-up eyes" (6).

The author also shares the trauma and post-traumatic stress disorder of Hassan's son Sohrab who is tormented in the captivity of Aseef. Sohrab is depicted as a helpless and hopeless child who is scared to the extent that he avoids eye contact with people. The trauma caused by the Taliban has left a deep scar on the mind of Sohrab such that he decides to give up his life instead of going back to the orphanage. He attempts to kill himself by slitting his veins using an old blade. However, he is saved by the Doctors and survives the attempt. Amir soon finds a way to adopt Sohrab and gives him a new home in California. Though he is safe with Amir, Sohrab still reflects post-traumatic stress disorder in his silence and numbness. Sohrab feels that his world has been destroyed and would never be the same again. He thinks that his home, people, and country are taken over by terror which will never remain the same as they used to be.

The Kite Runner is a narration of recovery that ends in happiness and hope. Though Hassan's recovery is not narrated in the novel, both Amir and Sohrab recover from their trauma. Amir's recovery happens as his body gets shattered in the fight with Asif. Between the immense pain, Amir laughs for the first time in years after Hassan's rape. The series of actions to correct his guilt led Amir to heal and redeem himself. Sohrab's situation demanded action from Amir, who fought Aseef to protect Sohrab from the clutches of the Taliban. Amir felt relieved amidst the intense physical pain because he knew that he had not sinned. Amir has stood up for his faiths, beliefs, and ethics.

Sohrab's recovery begins with the celebration of Afghan New Year when Amir offers a kite to Sohrab for him to fly. Sohrab remains aloof for some time but shatters his limitations to fly the kite along with Amir. He enjoys flying kite with Amir and cuts another kite. A smile escapes Sohrab's lips and Amir asks him if he wants Amir to run that kite for him. Though Sohrab did not respond Amir can read his expressions.

In the preface to the novel, Hosseini dedicates the novel to his children-Haris and Farah and to the children of Afghanistan. By employing child characters to speak of the trauma they experienced, Hosseini successfully conveys the message to children that they should treat trauma as a part of life. The way to be mature is to face trauma bravely, endeavour to remedy the faults and obtain personal redemption. In the novel, Amir describes seeing Hassan's face briefly immediately before Assef carries out his sexual assault. According to Amir, the look he witnessed there was one of "resignation" enough to bring Amir's mind to a similar look of resignation he witnessed on the face of a sheep on Eid as the mullah cut its throat. The narrative cuts away to a detailed description of this memory, effectively doubling on a structural level Amir's inability to process the scene as if unfolds. The horror of the recounting memory, with the violence it entails, allows Hassan to render his trauma via a conduit experience, thereby communicating devastation without forcing its articulation.

From childhood onwards, Amir goes through various issues which disturb his peace of mind. Because of being sensitive, Amir believes that he is being neglected by his father. Moreover, witnessing the sexual abuse of his close friend, separation from his mother, separation from Hassan, and life in an unstable environment have deeply impacted Amir's mind. His symptoms are insomnia, nightmares, guilt, shame, self-blame and grief. He is unable to cope with the situation well, and it is not until the end of the novel that he finally rids himself of his guilt.

The whole narration is a heart-clenching depiction of a gradual shift from the playful days of innocence and childhood to those of Hassan and Amir being a victim of childhood trauma; a childhood bully becoming the leader of the Taliban and tormenting children in the name of social supremacy. A significant part of the writing speaks of Amir's trauma and post-traumatic stress disorder as the narration is told in the first person. However, the author has successfully narrated the observations of the victim's trauma too. While Amir was struggling to deal with his guilt Hassan was struggling with the trauma resulting from being a rape victim. The Kite Runner is a reliable story that speaks of trauma, post-traumatic stress disorder, and recovery. In his writings, Khaled Hosseini effectively conveys the complexity of helplessness when haunted by the memories of childhood sexual abuse.

Collective trauma is a traumatic psychological effect shared by a group of people of any size up to and including an entire society. Traumatic events witnessed by an entire society can stir up collective sentiment, often resulting in a shift in the society's culture and mass actions. Besides the collective trauma brought by the war on Afghan society, what haunts the reader mostly is the collective trauma suffered by the Hazara community in the novel.

The Kite Runner is written in a way that a reader can easily become caught up in the class struggles between under-privileged Hazaras (minority) and comparatively affluent Pashtuns (majority). The collective trauma of the Hazaras originated from their inferior identities. They were discriminated against and oppressed in Afghanistan for many generations. As depicted in the novel, one day Amir found a history book with a chapter on Hazara history. From Amir's narration, the reader can get a glimpse of the history of the Hazara people:

In it, I read that my people, the Pashtuns, had persecuted and oppressed the Hazaras. It said the Hazaras had tried to rise against the Pashtuns in the nineteenth century, but the Pashtuns had "quelled them with unspeakable violence". The book said that my people had killed the Hazaras, driven them from their lands, burned their homes and sold their women. (8-9)

Such oppression can be clearly seen from the people's brutal treatment of Hassan and his father Ali: "They called him 'flat-nosed' because of Ali and Hassan's characteristic Hazara Mongoloid features .... School textbooks barely mentioned them and referred to their ancestry only in passing" (8). Through the voice of protagonist Amir, Hosseini also highlights the injustice and brutal reality. Amir contrasts his large house with Hassan's mud shack. He describes Hassan's mother as a "beautiful but notoriously unscrupulous woman who lives up to her dishonourable repetition" (7). On the contrary, Amir describes his own mother as "a highly educated woman universally regarded as one of Kabul's most respected, beautiful, and virtuous ladies" (15)Moreover, Amir describes Hassan's father to have monogamous features, which worsen with several physical disabilities. On the other hand, he describes his own father as"a towering Pashtun" (16).

Through Amir's stream of thoughts, readers can also perceive how some people from privileged classes in Kabul, would consider the racial and sectarian identity as external, as their fate: Never mind any of those things. Because history isn't easy to overcome. Neither is religion. In the end. I was a Pushtan and he was a Hazara, I was Sunni and he was Shia, and nothing was ever going to change that nothing(27). The racial attitude explains why Marc Forster's film *The Kite Runner*, based on the novel of the same name, is banned in Afghanistan. Afghanistan's government claims that the film presents the ethnic group in "a bad light", and therefore could trigger an ethnic and sectarian controversy.

But as a writer with responsibility, Hosseini is clearly aware that human being needs to understand the past in order to reclaim the present and the future.Through Hosseini's artistic creation, reader can realize the power of speaking the unspeakable and witness first-hand the creative energy that is presented in the novel. Besides the racial trauma of Hazaras, the collective trauma of war on Afghans, especially on Afghan children is also clearly represented in the novel. Here, the reader can find many haunting images of the war inflicted on the Afghan society: a man, desperate to feed his children, trying to sell his artificial leg in the market; an adulterous couple stoned to death in a stadium during the halftime of a football match: hanging body on the tree: and suicide on the way of escape. Death permeates every corner, as in the letter of Hassan to Amir, he points out that:

Alas! the Afghanistan of our youth is long dead. Kindness is gone from the land and you cannot escape the killings. Always the killings. In Kabul, fear is everywhere, in the struts, in the stadium, in the markets, it is a part of our lives here, Amir Agha (233).

The plight and trauma which the Hazaras have to face are clearly mentioned throughout the novel. The Hazaras were deprived of education and they were even not allowed to do any business of their own. They were constantly tormented by the majority group Pashtun. They have to work as the servants of Pashtun, like the way Hassan and his father Ali are doing for Amir's Family. Even the Afghan education systems perpetuate this discrimination. They are least concerned about including the history of the Hazara ethnic group in the syllabus. We know from the words of Amir, that in schools the history of Hazara is least mentioned.

Amir recalls how was the younger neighbourhood's kids hurt and insulted Hassan by calling him "flat nosed". Amir too cherishes his Pashtun idea of considering superior to Hassan despite the days and nights the two boys played together, despite the several adventure and explorations they have executed. Amir never thought of or mentioned Hassan as his friend. For him, Hassan was more of a playmate. Amir develops his feeling of superiority considering the relationship Baba keeps with Ali. Baba can be seen telling about his childhood with Ali and how they used to play together. But Baba nevertheless mentioned Ali as his good friend.

The discrimination towards Hazaras turned its most ugly face through the misdeed done by the Pashtun boy Assef towards Hassan. Assef wanted to beat up Amir for his friendship with Hassan, because he thought all the Hazaras should be eliminated from the country. The feelings of superiority are so included in his psyche that it finally developed into hatred. In his mind, Hassan and Hazaras are worthless and must be taught a lesson so he persists and rapes Hassan, an incident which shattered the minds of Hassan and Amir.

The Hazaras are portrayed as inferior to the Pushtans. When Amir and Baba escaped to Pakistan and then to California following the Soviet Union's military intervention in Afghanistan the house was left to Rahim Khan. Hassan and his wife were massacred by the Taliban, as they protested against the confiscation of the mansion by the troop. Hassan remained a loyal servant till his last breath. Hassan is just one such example of the direct persecution Hazaras face. He is the representative of the class as a whole. The novel also suggests that people need to act against the authoritative and intimidating power structures that try to dominate society through their oppressive norms. It suggests moving beyond the cultural, psychological and ethnic deadlocks and granting the right to dignity to the Afghan male children as well as the freedom to make choices for their betterment.

Hosseini's *The Kite Runner* finds a place as a trauma fiction by employing child characters to express the mental trauma they experience, the painful image of war and the racial and national trauma of Afghans. Hosseini successfully employs trauma as a personal and social phenomenon and thereby constructing restoration of social order and the healing of individual pain in current Afghan society.

WORKS CITED

Primary Source:

Hosseini, Khaled. *The Kite Runner*. 1st ed., Riverhead Books, 2013.

Secondary Source:

Caruth, Cathy. *Unclaimed Experience: Trauma, Narrative, and History.* Johns Hopkins University Press, 1996.

Freud, Sigmund. *Beyond the Pleasure Principle.* The International Psycho-Analytical Press, 1922.

Showalter, Elaine. *The Female Malady: Women, Madness, and English Culture, 1830-1980.* Pantheon Books, 1985.

Whitehead, Anne. *Trauma Fiction.* Edinburgh University Press, 2004.

CHAPTER XI

DIGITAL LEARNING AND PEDAGOGICAL IMPLICATION IN COVID-19 PANDEMIC TIMES

*Nandini Jyothiraj

Teacher Educant, Mahatma Gandhi University

Alappuzha, Kerala

The World awaited the 21st century with the aim of rapid technological development through structured pedagogical construction. However, the development and its reach were far from the realization of this aim. As per studies many public schools, as well as regional private schools, lacked sufficient technological infrastructure and proper know-how to entertain this rapid transition induced by the pandemic. For the first time in the history of mankind, the future of billions of students was at stake. The study analyses the parallel shift where technology has started to guide the construction of pedagogy in the new normal situation. This transient shift in the teaching-learning process is likely to initiate a significant change in a child's knowledge acquisition, character formation and skill development.

The study is centred on the teaching and learning process in Kerala during the pandemic. The study also revolves around the construction of a pedagogy where the students, students thought processes, understanding and curiosity can be honed and guided on the right track.

OBJECTIVES:

- To analyse the effectiveness of digital learning and internet connectivity in Kerala
- To study how far the teachers in Kerala are effective in conducting online classes
- To examine the learning gap that originated during the lockdown period in Kerala.

METHODOLOGY:

Observation and tertiary data analysis

INTRODUCTION

The 21st century began with the aim of rapid technological development through structured pedagogical construction. Schools and colleges slowly induce technology in syllabi by adopting IT and computer science as a subject. However, the development and its reach were far from the realization of this aim. The sudden crisis induced by pandemics in the year 2020 paved the way for rapid change. The spread of coronavirus forced state authorities to withdraw from all developmental activities including education. As per studies many public schools, as well as regional private schools, lacked sufficient technological infrastructure and proper know-how to entertain this rapid transition induced by the pandemic. For the first time in the history of mankind, the future of billions of students was at stake. The study analyses the parallel shift where technology has started to guide the construction of pedagogy in the new normal situation. This transient shift in the teaching-learning process is likely to initiate a significant change in a child's knowledge acquisition, character formation and skill development.

In India, many schools and colleges banned their students from the use of digital gadgets on campus. Ironically schools and colleges are now encouraging students to have digital gadgets for making education accessible. The dilemma faced by governmental authorities during digitalization was the lack of uniform and adequate network connectivity. The pandemic merely came with a solution. Now almost more than half of the students even in remote areas of villages have network connections for the purpose of access to education (even though its stability is still criticized and discussed). When digitalization brought education to doors it's the student who decides what to learn from the chunk of information provided through the sources like the internet. This is what millions of teachers and educational authorities have to brainstorm about. Proper construction of pedagogy is the need of the hour where the students thought processes, understanding and curiosity can be honed and guided on the right track. The question which is to be answered is, - "How can this challenge be faced by our educational authorities?"

EFFECTIVENESS OF DIGITAL TEACHING-LEARNING AND INTERNET CONNECTIVITY IN KERALA

Ever since March 2020 schools in Kerala were shut down due to the Pandemic. Classes since then have been conducted online. The major challenge faced by the authorities as well as the government was the inadequacy of network connectivity. Several students in different parts of Kerala found it difficult to attend classes online due to a lack of internet facilities, resources and other financial constraints.

Most private schools resumed their higher secondary classes in the month of May through online platforms like ZOOM, TEAMS and GOOGLE MEET while public schools aired their classes through the VICTORS channel and the web. After four months of lockdown in June 2020, the

Department of Women and Child Development, Kerala launched a programme "Kilikonchal" to ensure preschool education of children.

Even though the government had taken initiatives to make education feasible, the benefit did not reach the targeted group partially if not fully. It was found that many children were not able to watch the programme as they did not have a TV or internet facility at home. For a sizable part of the targeted group, it was the lack of adequate signal strength that kept them from accessing the lessons.

The government has taken various measures like providing educational kits to students to avoid backlags and dropouts. The Kerala Infrastructure Technology for Education (KITE) under the auspices of the General Education Department has set up a platform in collaboration with the Google Workspace for teaching-learning. The government has also formed a nineteen-member committee to implement the 'LET'S GO DIGITAL' project to ensure a learning management system based on MOODLE to all institutions which would provide the necessary cloud to impart training to teachers and students in digital learning and to set up smart classes in all institutions. Yet the success of online education is in a dilemma.

TEACHING-LEARNING GAP

Other than network connectivity, infrastructural inefficiency and financial instability the main issue faced is lack of interaction, proper communication and psychological instability among students as well as educators. The pandemic has not only challenged the teachers but also the students.

The physical presence of a teacher is being replaced by a computer screen. And for teachers, the students are mere profile pictures. Discipline, socialization, punctuality, regularity, obedience and all such values which are inculcated in a student during school life are now slowly getting endangered. The online mode has created a greater gap between student-teacher, parent-teacher and student-student. Children have now turned easier going. They fear no punishments and online mode has made them escape from regular classes with an excuse of lack of network.

Online teaching has also affected the health of students as they have for the past eighteen months or so been concentrating more on computer screens without any physical activity. Some of the schools overburdened the students by giving more and more online activities and home works on the excuse that they have more time at hand than they used to when they attend regular classes at school. This too has had a negative impact on the mental health of the students.

The pedagogic inputs have not been sufficiently provided to the students through this media and the assessment of the student community – the learning outcome - has become extremely vulnerable. The achievement level of the entire student has drastically declined during this period. Moreover, the syllabus was also shortened by the decision-makers in education for overcoming the catastrophe inflicted by the pandemic.

PUPIL WITH DISABILITY

The most vulnerable in the student community has been the pupil with disability (PwD). Little could be done to help the visually impaired, the hearing impaired and the mentally and physically challenged. Many schools, where inclusive education was the practice could do little to help such pupils. The burden of continuing education fell on the untrained shoulders of the parents. Both the Centre and the State governments too could do nothing to help the PwD continue their education during the academic year 2020-2021. Availing the course materials in the 'sign language' and 'the audio books' by the CBSE; in collaboration with the NCERT has taken a huge leap into marking history and making the future of such children.

FINDINGS:

- Lockdown inflicted a serious learning gap amongst students in Kerala
- Persistent poor connectivity and ill-equipped digital infrastructure
- Creation of a greater gap between student-teacher, parent-teacher and student-student
- Learning outcomes and achievement levels of students have gone down
- The mental health of the students was affected negatively
- The needs of the PwD were not catered to
- The success of online education is in dilemma

CONCLUSION

The pandemic has taken a toll on all the activities of the world. Education is at stake. As per my study crisis has encouraged the school system to adapt to the new teaching and learning norm. Even though the lockdown has inflicted a serious learning gap amongst the students, teachers to an extent have tried to maintain the quality of education and encouraged students to uphold their learning curiosity.

WORKS CITED

"Classes on VICTERS channel from June 1." *The Hindu*, Kerala, 26 May. 2021 https://www.thehindu.com/news/national/kerala/classes-on-victers-channel-from-june-1/article34650945.ece/amp/. Accessed 27 July 2021.

"Kerala: Regular online classes from Monday." The Times of India, 19 June. 2021 https://timesofindia.indiatimes.com/city/thiruvananthapuram/kerala-regular-online classes-from-Monday/articles how/83659085.cms. Accessed 26 July 2021.

Priyo, Asad Karim Khan, UmmahaHazra. "Digital divide in online class during Covid-19 pandemic." *The Financial Express*, Tuesday, 3 August 2021 https://thefinancialexpress.com.bd/views/opinions/digital-divide-in-online-class-during covid-19-pandemic-1626620177?amp=true. Accessed 27 July 2021.

9 798887 491851

Printed by Libri Plureos GmbH in Hamburg, Germany